Al Smith
and
His America

Oscar Handlin

Al Smith
and
His America

With a New Foreword by the
Author

Northeastern University Press • *Boston*

First Northeastern University Press edition 1987

Library of Congress Cataloging-in-Publication Data

Handlin, Oscar, 1915–
Al Smith and his America.
Reprint. Originally published: Boston : Little, Brown,
1958.
Includes index.
1. Smith, Alfred Emanuel, 1873–1944. 2. Presidential
candidates—United States—Biography. 3. New York (State)—
Governors—Biography. 4. Presidents—United States—
Election—1928. 5. United States—Politics and government—
1919–1933. I. Title.
E748.S63H16 1987   973.91'5'0924 [B]   87-15235
ISBN 1-55553-021-4 (pbk.: alk. paper)

Printed and bound by Courier Co., Westford, Mass. The
paper is Glatfelter Offset, an acid-free sheet.

MANUFACTURED IN THE UNITED STATES OF AMERICA
96 95 94 93 92   5 4 3 2

To
Arthur H. Cole

Contents

Author's Preface

On both sides of the Atlantic, in the eighteenth and ninetenth centuries a vision took hold of men's imaginations, a vision so close to reality as to be utterly convincing.

America was the promised land, the society of open opportunity, where every man, whatever his background or origin, could move to the place to which ability entitled him. The poor could grow rich, the weak powerful and the humble proud if their talents justified it. The lad born in the log cabin could some day dwell in the White House.

No matter that the dream was not altogether true to life — inherited wealth and distinguished parentage did make a difference — still it was true enough to lead on, in faith, the millions of Europeans who became Americans. To the immigrants and to their children this was the most hopeful aspect of life in the United States. They could not escape the contrast with the society they had left behind in which status was rigidly fixed and opportunity confined to a fortunate few. Here the whole community profited through finding the abilities it needed when and where it needed them.

So much greater, therefore, was the shock to discover as the twentieth century opened that artificial barriers to opportunity were being raised in contravention of these ideals. The challenge to the traditional conceptions of equality and opportunity produced a dark episode in American history. Al Smith, who lived through it, was peculiarly its victim. The society which miraculously opened to him his greatest opportunity spitefully tripped him up when he attempted to seize it.

The buoyant optimism of Americans has often deceived them into thinking that their whole history was one great success story. Yet the failures have, in their own way, been as significant and as important as the successes. The life of Alfred E. Smith had a full measure of both.

OSCAR HANDLIN

Foreword to the 1987 Edition

THE FIRST EDITION of this book, which appeared in 1958, made a sharp impression on then-Senator John F. Kennedy of Massachusetts. The question it raised troubled the young legislator. Could a Catholic be elected president of the United States?

The future president was struck by the way in which the book described Al Smith's conviction that "partisanship and political compromise are essential ingredients of American politics." Kennedy also was impressed with Smith's "unusual capacity to face and absorb facts and to mobilize talents from the professions and universities." Most of all he was struck by the issue of Catholicism. It seemed to him that during the 1920s there was a special set of factors unlikely to be repeated in the same combination or intensity in his own day. The revolt against Smith, he believed, was a fundamentalist rebellion that grew out of a nativist consciousness, all of which interrelated so that it was clear that Catholicism by itself was not the cause of Smith's defeat. Kennedy's own political experience convinced him that this factor had been considerably mitigated.

There were indeed reasons for the focus on religion as a divisive element in American life in the decades after the first world war. The changing society and the novel challenges of a new world order led to a reaction—an inward sense that drove people toward isolation and toward the reassertion of old verities. That made many Americans fundamentalists in 1928 and their anti-Catholicism affected the outcome of the presidential election that year. The discussion that follows demonstrates that religion was not an isolated factor in the decade of the 1920s but rather was intimately linked to attitudes toward the city, toward foreigners, and toward the prohibition amendment; and Al Smith represented to many the totality of alien forces undermining the country. His defeat therefore stood for a reassertion of values threatened by change.

In the years after the second world war, the pattern of prejudice changed. The old America, weakened by depression, then vanished—and along with it earlier forms of intergroup relationships. Race became a stronger divisive element than religion; and the forces pressing toward adjustment leveled the distance between Catholicism and other faiths in the United States. By the time Kennedy considered his own candidacy, the intellectual and social landscape had changed.

In retrospect, the author finds it difficult to judge the extent to which those factors influenced the writing of this book. To some commentators it seemed in 1958 a tract for the times. But it was actually conceived and much of it written in 1951, long before John F. Kennedy harbored presidential ambitions. Yet the record of both failure and achievement this book outlines is not without relevance in the 1980s any more than in the 1950s.

Since the first publication of this volume, renewed interest in the ethnic elements in American history has generated considerable useful scholarship bearing upon the progressive period in American politics. Those works, however, have not required revision of the interpretations advanced here. Nor has it been necessary to deal with two substantive matters, both conjectural—the first suggesting that one of Smith's grandparents was Italian, the second that wealthy friends arranged for his financial support. Both possibilities are interesting and not implausible; but neither is fully proven and neither would call for revision of the account given here.

November 1986   O. H.

Al Smith
and
His America

I

A Stage for Life

CAN A CATHOLIC ever be President of the United States?

That was the gist of the article by Charles C. Marshall in the April 1927 issue of the *Atlantic Monthly,* although the actual title ran, "An Open Letter to the Honorable Alfred E. Smith."

Now, as the Governor of New York looked at his own response in the May issue of the magazine, he had cause for satisfaction. Enormous public interest had been generated in the interval. The Boston *Post* had gone to the length of stealing an advance number to score a beat, the *Atlantic* had been rushed by special trucks to New York to assure prompt distribution, and every important newspaper in the nation had reprinted the statement. No doubt that was all to the good for a man who hoped to run for the presidency the following year. And perhaps this answer might still the questioners.

Yet in his heart Al Smith felt a deep uneasiness. Could any answer, no matter how convincing or logical, satisfy those who ought never to have asked the question in the first place?

Earlier that year, he had already rejected Franklin Roosevelt's suggestion that he defend the patriotism of Catholics in the pages of the *Independent*. No defense was necessary, Al indignantly rejoined. And when his friend, Joe Proskauer, had brought around the proofs of the April *Atlantic*, Smith's response had been the same. "I've been a devout Catholic all my life and I never heard of these bulls and encyclicals and books." All that had nothing to do with it. What was relevant was the individual and his conscience and, above all, the record he had made. The endless quibbling about theory had no importance.

In the end, Smith, with the aid of Judge Proskauer and Father Duffy, had composed the reply. But for all its eloquence and sincerity, the Governor never ceased to wonder whether it had made as good a case for him as had the practical achievements of his own life.

For almost a decade he had been chief executive of the nation's largest state. He had confronted and had solved the problems of governing an industrial, urban community. The battles he had fought and won were still fresh in people's minds — battles over power and education and social justice. He could in earnest say, in 1927, that he had helped make the state not only honest and efficient but also an instrument to serve the welfare of its citizens.

The ability he had displayed in those ten years had not come from theories, but from the experience of an active life. Even back in 1915, amidst all the learned men who had assembled in a great constitutional convention, he had demonstrated the superiority of the knowledge derived from participation in events over that derived from books. He could think back in his own career to the slow unfolding of the understanding of what government was, through service in the legislature, and of what government was for, through his exposure to the people's problems after the tragic Triangle fire of 1911.

And even earlier, before he really knew anything, he had been part of a society and had learned from its ways of acting what Americanism meant. Many years had passed, and he had come a long way since he had carried his boy's dreams through the teeming streets of New York's East Side. Yet the faith nurtured there remained strong: that beneath their external conditions all men were equal. That was the valid response to those who challenged his religion. When the memory came back of the stirring lines he had once declaimed and still believed, he had no doubt but that the American people would some day realize that his reply to Marshall was but the needless spelling out of what his life had already said more eloquently.

In the parish club theatricals, the earnest young man always took a prominent part. He loved the play-acting, the opportunity to speak the resounding, sentimental sentences, and the applause. Often, he thought, the make-believe world of the stage was the most important part of his life.

It was true he never liked to take the villain's role. He wished the audience to identify itself with him; if he could but be their spokesman, say what they wanted to hear, why then he would be sure to feel them always on his side. That was what he wanted most — to have them on his side. Perhaps that was why, although he sometimes thought of it, he never made the effort to move on to the professional theater. It was more comfortable — and for

him more rewarding — to play his part within the con-
fines of the intimate little world in which he lived.

That world was wedged into a great and growing metropolis. But it had a coherence and an identity of its own.
Outside the boundaries was a larger universe, occupied by
multitudes unknown and incomprehensible to one another, and frightening in its strangeness. Within the limits
of the familiar world was the security of known relationships. Here was the adequate fixed center of a man's life.
Much of his character was shaped here.

The Battery section of the Fourth Ward of New York
was not large geographically. A man could easily walk
from the East River westward to the Bowery, from South
Street northward to East Broadway. Yet these narrow
streets, lined by a motley array of tenements, of converted
warehouses, of dwellings in every stage of repair and decay,
and of shacks and shanties, housed a whole universe, primarily Irish in its constitution.

Mostly it had acquired its character in the great wave
of immigration that swept across the Atlantic between
1840 and 1860. The presence of the Irish had begun to
make itself felt in the city long before. But it was only
toward the middle of the century that the Emerald Isle
entered upon the convulsions that shifted millions of its
residents to the United States. A rising population and an
archaic land system, the shortsightedness and selfishness of
the rulers of the land, and a stagnant economy compelled
a mounting number of displaced peasants to emigrate.
Then the great potato famine of 1846 completed the
process. In the face of that overwhelming disaster, whoever
could, fled. In two tragic decades more than two million

of them left home. For almost all of them, there was but one refuge, the United States.

Many of the refugees came to New York City, the greatest Atlantic port. Without resources as they straggled off the ships, they were more likely than not to settle in the East Side. There they found cheap housing close to the wharves where they sought work; and there they began the laborious process of reconstructing their shattered lives. Few brought with them the skills or capital required to advance far in America. Mostly they were condemned to the poverty-stricken role of day laborers and the harsh existence that that marginal position afforded them.

Quickly the district filled up. The Fourth Ward, in its center, held 11,000 inhabitants in 1835; fifteen years later its population had doubled. The neighboring wards along the East River also attracted the Irish and also grew rapidly.

The facilities of the quarter could not expand as quickly as the newcomers crowded into it. Here and there, as on Dover Street, low gable-roofed houses survived from a time when Dutch burghers had looked out upon a country lane. But inexorably the tenements spread throughout these wards. Under the pressure of overcrowding, all standards of housing deteriorated and the older inhabitants hurriedly moved away. Indeed, as living conditions grew worse, there was a perpetual turnover among the district's residents; those who achieved the means to do so departed and left it to the poor and the newly arrived.

The East Side early acquired an unsavory reputation. Close to the waterfront, it played host to the rowdy sailor element as well as to more respectable guests who sought there diversions not available uptown. Across the Bowery was a district of ill repute, where saloons, gambling rooms, music halls and houses of prostitution furnished a variety of amusements. This was an atmosphere conducive to crime and vice.

The hard-working immigrants struggled to keep themselves isolated from these surroundings. They developed their own communal institutions and sought to hold together in their difficulties as if they were still in the village back across the ocean, and not in a great, strange, hostile city.

The mothers and fathers knew in a vague way of the evils in the midst of which they lived and they tried to warn off their children from the wickedness of the well-to-do. It was not easy, of course, amidst the poverty and overcrowding, to teach the young ones the difference between right and wrong. Sure and sometimes a small boy, walking with his father, might pass through the swinging doors of a beer hall and look and listen curiously while his elders passed a half-hour. But still he was made to know what was decent and proper so that he would not grow up to be one of those men without standards who frequented the bad places that were all about. Against heavy odds, the immigrants were remarkably successful in detaching their own communities from the disorderly life of the district.

Alfred Emanuel Smith had been born into one of the Oliver Street families in about 1840. The exact details of his parentage, or even of the date of his birth, faded into the ill-recorded history of the poor. He grew up within the limited range of opportunities of his environment. As he matured he moved from one job to another — none highly paid, none involving skill. He was a good man, a member of a volunteer fire company; and he had enlisted in the Civil War with the "Bowery Boys." Loyal to his friends, he remained a faithful, quiet man. By the time he was thirty his first wife had died and had left him with the care of a small daughter. Easygoing, he continued to live close to the spot on which he had been born.

Among his neighbors were Thomas and Maria Mulvehill. In 1841, a sixty-day crossing on the Black Ball Line had brought them from Westmeath in Ireland. They had landed at the foot of Beekman Street and they too never moved far from the point of their initial contact with the New World. At the corner of Dover and Water Streets they lived above a little grocer's shop and reared a family.

In September 1872 Smith married their daughter Catherine, ten years his junior. They settled at 174 South Street; and there, on December 30, 1873, was born their only son, named Alfred Emanuel Smith for his father.

The little boy grew up in America's largest city. But the neighborhood that shaped him was a small world of its own. Living on the top floor of the narrow house, he could run through the four rooms of the flat and look out of the window of the front room. The cobbled streets were dirty; not until he was a grown man would the "whitewings" make an effort to keep them clean. But the animated life of those streets was an education in itself.

Or, he could wander downstairs, loiter by Mr. Morgenweck's barbershop on the second floor, peep in at the fruit store on the ground floor, and make his way out into the bustle of Oliver Street. If he got over to Water Street on a weekday he found endless fascination in the turmoil of shouting teamsters guiding their great trucks along the narrow ways. On Sunday the same street, grown quiet and empty, offered opportunity for play, heedless of the strays who sang restlessly in the mission on the corner. The gaslit evenings had a magic of their own, as the men returned from work took their leisure in the out-of-doors; and all the world, for the moment, were loiterers.

The whole waterfront was a playground, with the docks places of endless wonder. A boy could swim in the river or hide among the stacked-up crates or climb in the rigging of the ships. Strange sailors and their pets made thrilling acquaintances. For a time, Al kept a West Indian goat, four dogs, a parrot and a monkey in the attic at home.

Sometimes Al would go down to where the Brooklyn Bridge was rising magically out of the waters and look away to the far distance on the other side. Occasional excursions took him to remote places; at the age of four he stands in a picture at Coney Island, a pail clutched tightly in his right hand, looking hesitantly outward at the larger world. But mostly he came to know the sights and sounds of the streets of his home. Goodhearted outsiders who wandered into the Fourth Ward and knew, or thought they knew, the abominations of its alleys shuddered at the effects upon children of a scene "which even to look upon for a fleeting instant carries pollution with it." Such observers could not understand that, for boys like Al, the district had its own saving influences.

Not far away was the Roman Catholic Church of St. James. The Smiths were devout communicants. Their ancestral faith, brought by their parents from the Old World, had become an integral part of their lives in the New. Religion for them was not simply a matter of pas-

sive identification. It involved a set of deeply held beliefs
that explained man's place in the world; and it demanded
of its adherents active participation in a round of activities
that filled important parts of their lives. The men, the
women, and the children too had all their roles in a
community which, like a village, clustered about the
church.

In 1879, when Al was five years old, Father John Kean
became the pastor of St. James's. A vigorous, forceful man,
he assumed the charge of the eighteen thousand souls in
the parish and began at once to vitalize their association
with it. He built up a complex pattern of societies that
were intended to occupy and involve the faithful of every
age. It was good to find here clubs to which the young ones
could go and friends who could help out with a job or
advice when needed.

Al was a good lad, taught by his mother to be attentive
to his duties. He was not to grow up wild like the raga-
muffins who disgraced the neighborhood. Neatly dressed,
indeed on Sundays polished and starched, he showed
visible evidence of his good upbringing. An immaculate
appearance was even more important for the children of
the slums than for the well-to-do as a sign of respectability;
and the habit of careful attention to his clothing would
remain with Al through life.

For him, as for any other decent fellow, the Church
early became exceedingly important. Before he had
reached the age of ten he was an altar boy and, morning
after morning, appeared in time to serve at the seven
o'clock Mass. For years he pumped the organ for Annie
Rush, and he was a dutiful if not illustrious scholar in the
school conducted by the Christian Brothers.

He was not to have the opportunity for studies very long. His father's earnings were always small, with hardly a margin for emergencies; that was the condition of most of the men in the Fourth Ward. At the age of eleven, Al already felt the obligation to take up a newsboy's stand to contribute his share to the family's income. A year later, in 1886, his father died after a long illness, and a prolonged crisis set in. His mother, who had worked earlier, returned to the umbrella factory on Madison Street. Often the lad could see her toil on into the night for the extra pay home work brought in. He himself left school and became an active wage earner.

He drifted through a variety of positions. For two years he earned three dollars a week as a chaser for William J. Redmond, a truckman of the neighborhood. Al scouted for business and he directed the carts to jobs as they came in. Then he moved upward to eight dollars as a laborer in an oil factory; and for three years he put in a twelve-hour day that began at 4 A.M. to earn his twelve dollars a week at the Fulton Fish Market. By 1895 he was employed in a pump works in Brooklyn.

He was then twenty-one, but still without a clear goal in life. Nothing had thus far distinguished Al from thousands of his fellows. As he rose at six each morning to take the ferry across the river, he might well have reflected that he certainly could go on as he had begun, go on as his father had, in a humdrum round of acts without purpose, to marry and beget children who would remember him with vague affection after the wearying drudgery of ill-paid labor took him away.

Except that Al dreamed of something more; and even

within the ambit of his own little world he could discern the openings of avenues of escape.

The boys could make their way down by the Chatham Street clothing stores to the Bowery where the German shops were. They could stand near the dime museums and joke curiously about the freaks. They could peep in by the bars of the beer or concert halls at the tiny stages on which existed a resplendent merry world of song and dance. Or they could find places in the theater's gallery and rock with laughter at the variety comic or give way to unashamed grief at the tribulations of the tragic heroine.

This was certainly a way out. In the face of the bright lights and the gay colors, the dreary life of every day receded. There was magic in the antics of the acrobats and irony in the lyrics and drama in the action. And as the wondrous meaning of it all caught the audience up, it moved them to tumultuous applause, to cheers and jeers and shouted advice that demonstrated their participation in the world of the stage.

At Niblo's Garden on Prince Street, Al had seen his first play: Kit Chanfran in *The Arkansas Traveler*. Thereafter he was an inveterate theatergoer. Harrigan and Hart, Sam Bernard, David Warfield, Maggie Kline, Pat Rooney, Weber and Fields, and Fanny Davenport — these were the stars that enlivened his nights. And the memories made easier days that were full of toil.

Al's dreams, however, cast him not simply as one of the watchers, but as an actor in the play.

From earliest youth he had been eager to speak out, to stand forth upon the platform and declaim the resounding sentences that touched the emotions — to let drop the quips that moved listeners to laughter. The anxiety to be heard was not the product of vanity. It expressed rather the deeply felt need for an audience. In the magic of the stage transformation the actor became the character. That was why Smith never at any point in his life relished the role of villain. He was uncomfortable in empty gestures, in anything less than the certainty that he actually was what the part made him.

That was also why he needed a meaningful relationship with his fellows on the other side of the footlights. The applause and the laughter were a kind of assurance that he, Al, was not alone, detached, but bound in somehow in a communion of common action.

At only one exercise in his abbreviated school career had he at all distinguished himself. The elocution medal he brought back from a city-wide contest already showed the bent of his talents. With the kids on the block, he played at amateur theatricals in the attic, recapturing as actors the excitement of the dramas they had witnessed as spectators. Later, as a young man, he took a leading role in the St. James Lyceum Company, practicing and performing in the basement of the church. Never would he forget the sense of exhilaration as the eight hundred people who crowded into the makeshift auditorium sighed and laughed with him.

Sometimes too he would go down to take a place as a supernumerary in the ambitious presentations of the Windsor Theater on the Bowery. The glitter of the atmosphere, though he was but a lowly "supe," kept him dreaming of the glories of the actor's career.

Then he came to a turning and took another avenue, but the memories of this one never faded. Often later he would think back to the excitement of the dramas of which he had been a part, and with little urging would declaim the favorite passages for his friends: *The Ticket-of-Leave Man, The Lost Paradise, Incog,* and Dion Boucicault's heartwarming story of the Old Land, *The Shaughraun.*

But none was as dear to him, then or later, as *The Mighty Dollar.*

This little farce had long been identified with the rollicking Irish comic William Jermyn Florence. Billy Florence was, in 1890, established and famous enough to have ventured out into authorship. His *Gentlemen's Handbook on Poker* and his *Fables* sold well in the great audience whose favorite he was. Certainly any young man with acting in his blood envied Florence the esteem and admiration he had won.

Yet he too had once been but a poor Irish lad. Back before the Civil War his name had been Conlin, and he had shifted about from job to job playing the standard tipsy-jolly Irish clown. Then he had married the sister-in-law of the peerless Barney Williams and the two of them had put over a successful Mr. and Mrs. act. Finally, *The Mighty Dollar,* which he had presented for the first time at the Park Theater in 1875, earned him fame and fortune.

The play had been written expressly for him by Benjamin E. Woolf, one of the little-known hacks who then turned out the conventional scripts of the popular stage. Billy Florence achieved enormous success in the role of the good-humored but unscrupulous Congressman Bardwell Slote. It served him for more than ten years. The inconsequential plot involved a boy and girl in love, a railroad's effort to do the worthy hero out of his heritage, and a comic Englishman. Central to it all, however, was the character of Bardwell Slote.

P.D.Q., pretty darn quick, Slote was Johnny O.S. (on the spot). Unpretentious, his slang came straight from the heart. There was "too much 'highfalutin' " at the ball to which he had been invited; he preferred down-to-earth talk outside. Suspicious of the snobs whose ancestors came over on the *"Cauliflower,"* he condemned "what they call society! I'd like to have a contract to supply society with all the powder and paint it uses. It would beat a government contract by a large majority."

By some standards, Bardwell Slote might have been judged corrupt. But he was not so A.G. (awful green). "It is an F.F., a financial fact," he explained, "that the concern must be run on a cash basis." A man should serve his country well, but should also have "sense enough to see that his country rewarded him well for it." He was indignant that newspapers should "stick their noses into people's private affairs," and complain "when a patriotic Congressman tries to look after his own interests by a practical arrangement with some ambitious railroad."

This was close enough to life to be fun. And yet the make-believe of the stage dissolved the necessity for wondering whether or not it was true.

In any case, the happy ending resolves all conflict. Virtue is rewarded; the hero gets the heroine; and Slote exits with both the money and the honor. As the curtain begins to fall, the businessman assures him: "I shall not forget you, nor that we have had many interests in common, and if I can aid you to climb the political ladder you may rely upon my support, even to the presidential chair."

"And that's where I am going to land, by a large majority," answers Slote.

And the visiting Englishman just has time to comment:

"One of the remarkable conditions of a new country, that the road is open to him, and a man may be my employee today, and my president in the future."

But whether it was of Bardwell Slote he spoke, or of Billy Florence, or of Al Smith, the young man who took joy in the play was not yet sure.

I I

The Business of
Government

To THE BOYS who grew up in the Fourth Ward, politics was always in the center of life. It was not a thing apart, not a concern of strangers, but an intimate activity of their own society.

From far back in childhood, Al remembered the discussions of his father and uncle, as they sat in leisurely conversation and argued about the merits of the various chieftains struggling for power in the district. The stories of the great meetings, of the street brawls, of the tactical raids and maneuvers fed the imagination and lingered in the memory.

Like many other lads, too, Al loved to lounge about the firehouse on John Street, where politics was the staple of conversation. The members of the company talked endlessly of the exploits of the leaders. The question of who controlled the government was vital to the welfare of men whose very jobs depended upon the answer. But in addition, they were all absorbed in the sport of it. The turbulent contests for office held the same interest as baseball or boxing. These were all games that pitted champion against champion and let the best man win. The periodic struggles for power involved the loyalties of every resident in the Ward and permeated their lives with excitement.

Al's ambition then was to be a fireman like his Uncle Peter; and when he was somewhat older, he became a member of the Buffaloes, an informal group of youngsters who ran errands for their elders and made themselves otherwise useful when the cause demanded it.

Such services were good. They gave the boys a sense of participation in a common effort. As they listened to the resounding oratory of Bourke Cockran or later of Senator Tom Grady, "the silver-tongued orator of Tammany Hall," they were moved, as in the theater, by the drama of the struggle between us and them, between the good and the bad. And Al, just as he imitated his heroes of the stage, clipped and memorized Cockran's resounding sentences.

Acting in the group, the men acquired a morality of loyalty; the right fellow was the one who held to his pals against the hostile outsiders, rewarded service and punished betrayal, and was square in dealings with his peers. The loyal member was prepared to lend a helping hand to his fellows. No one was so secure that he could rely upon himself alone. A man was not a man, Al as a boy had heard his father say, if he was not able to do a favor for a friend.

To be one of the group was also to accept its rules as laid down by the leader. Once, when Al was seventeen, the St. James Union had a dispute with the priest, who had made an unpopular demand upon the club. Smith urged his friends to give in; if they were a part of the Church, they had to submit to it. For without authority and direction there was no order in life.

The same went for politics. "When the voters elect a man leader," one of the boys later explained, "they make a sort of a contract," although "it ain't written out." They put him there to look out for their interests, "to see that this district gets all the jobs that's comin' to it." In return they agree to be faithful. If "he spends most of his time chasin' after places in the departments, picks up jobs from railroads and contractors for his followers, and shows himself a true statesman," then they are bound to uphold him. Otherwise they are justified in rebellion. They may "up and swat him without bein' put down as political ingrates."

Down around Oliver Street there was no question as to who was the boss. Tom Foley, by every standard of the district, was indeed the man. From his earliest childhood, Smith could recall the burly figure striding down the block, the friendly smile behind the big black mustache, and the largess tossed to the children on the way. "A penny looked big" in those days, and "when you got a nickel you thought it was Sunday." And no boy growing up in the Fourth Ward could forget the pleasures of Foley's annual outings up in the country at Harlem.

Foley had come to New York from Ireland in 1872. He was then about twenty years old and had made his start as a blacksmith. A few years later he acquired a saloon at the corner of Oliver and Water Streets, a block away from Smith's home. Here the men came in after work or after supper for a leisurely glass. In the bright, warm place they talked idly in groups, or now and then burst into song. The atmosphere was always cheerful.

When Al became old enough to be dropping in of an

evening, Foley was in charge of an election precinct in the district of which Big Tim Sullivan was general over-lord. Tom had no ambitions to hold office, although he would in his lifetime serve briefly as alderman and sheriff. He was in politics for the love of the fight and for the power winning might give him. It was the saloon that was his domain.

Being the type of man he was, he was given to little acts of kindness. He was ever generous when his friends came to him for advice, assistance, and for intercession in the difficult world in which they lived. If it was a basket of coal that was needed in the winter, or a few dollars to bury some poor devil and take care of his widow, if there were trouble with the police or a job to be found, Foley was the man to see. And then there were the good times, the chowder parties and ox roasts, and balls and picnics that were the reward of being in with him.

In return, they were expected to bring out the vote on which political power rested. And wasn't it to their own advantage to do so, seeing as it was Tom who, through his connections, knew who would act in their interests and who would not!

Smith was a regular attendant at the saloon. He enjoyed the company of the men, and was anxious to be liked. Then too, it was a good idea to be around and available, if Foley should need someone to run an errand or help out in any way. Everyone knew it was one of the tasks of a leader to single out promising young men who might go far.

Here often Al would meet Henry Campbell, a some-what older fellow whom he also knew from St. James's. Campbell was better off than most, a wholesale grocer and an owner of real estate, and he now and then took the likable younger man home for Sunday dinner. In 1894, through his agency, Al found his way into a more active political role.

That was the year the lid blew off downtown. From the days of the Tweed ring onward, there had been periodic investigations of corruption in municipal government. But the revelations, as in 1884, had largely been of honest graft. And what if the aldermen got something for themselves for voting a streetcar franchise? They saw their opportunities and they took them, like the businessmen with whom they dealt. One of them made the ethics of it clear: "Supposin' it's a new bridge they're goin' to build. I get tipped off and I buy as much property as I can that has to be taken for approaches. I sell at my own price later on and drop some more money in the bank. Wouldn't you? It's just like looking ahead in Wall Street or in the coffee or cotton market." That might outrage the tender sensibilities of the uptowners. But no one really suffered thereby; and often it indirectly helped the poor folk in the district.

The new exposures were different. In 1892 the Reverend Henry Parkhurst had come down to Cherry Street and Park Row. He had looked in at the dives that openly flouted the law, and had witnessed the police in frank alliance with gamblers, prostitutes, and criminals. For two years his accusations had agitated the city. This, he proclaimed, was a "forcing room of crime" where the "cast-off scum" of Europe and America gathered to mark their ballots for Tammany Hall and corruption. Now a reform ticket was in the field with a candidate of its own in the mayoralty election.

The self-respecting men who gathered in Foley's knew that they were no cast-off scum, and they were inclined to take reformers' charges with a grain of salt. But they were uncomfortable in the knowledge that there was something to Parkhurst's revelations. A bit of boodle was one thing; but it was something else again to find the police pushing their own people around or to learn how their daughters were being drawn into prostitution.

This uneasiness meshed in with a local source of resentment. Croker up at the Hall had sent orders to the district leader, Big Tim Sullivan, that they were to have a new Congressman, and a man from outside the district at that. Henry Campbell, for one, resented this dictation from above. He knew that politics often made strange bedfellows and that the private in the ranks did not always understand the tactical maneuvers of the general. But it was not right that a good fellow should thus capriciously be set aside. Al Smith agreed; and one night over at Timothy J. Sullivan's Oriental Club on Grand Street he felt moved to rise and deliver his first political oration. He was just under twenty-one and not yet eligible to vote; but he was learning something about the connection of the Fourth Ward with the rest of the city.

Tammany carried off the nomination. But the incumbent Congressman bolted, and Smith and Campbell supported him. The revolt was futile. The bolters indirectly helped to elect a reform mayor, they lost the congressional race and they earned the enmity of the Democratic organization. Smith nevertheless had made his mark in the campaign. Campbell was convinced this was a lad to be watched and early in 1895 secured him a place as subpoena server in the Office of the Commissioner of Jurors. For the next nine years he would earn close to a thousand dollars a year. He was out of the laborers' rut.

The glitter of opportunity now unfolded before him. Why, it was a great and growing city and every man could make his way in it. Here was an empty lot or a battered shack; next year a tall building occupied the place and someone had made a fortune. Why, you could see it before your very eyes, spreading and growing and pulsing with the life of hidden wealth. So here was he, Al Smith, having dinner on St. Patrick's Day at Cahill's on Park Place. But sure as fate there would be a day when he would be sitting uptown with the Friendly Sons of St. Patrick along with the others who had come out on top. And what better way than politics for a lad to get there, who could work, and talk, and make friends.

Politics now became central to his interests, although he continued to act in his spare time. He attached himself to the Seymour Club and dropped in regularly at Foley's saloon. Sure Divver and the machine were out to get him for his insurgency. But he could bide his time and he could learn. Young Smith stood with the big crowds in Madison Square, when Bryan came by in 1896; and he followed the career of Teddy Roosevelt, the rough rider who became governor and then President. Al listened to the campaign oratory and he began to clip, and to paste into a scrapbook, editorial discussions of the issues of the day. Here was a glimmer of comprehension that there were aspects to politics other than the struggle for power.

He was by now familiar throughout the district. He began to dress more elegantly, took to smoking cigars and had himself photographed in a top hat. He bought a bicycle and occasionally used it to ride out to Far Rockaway and Coney Island. More and more often he went to the Bronx, where Miss Catherine Dunn lived on Third Avenue at 170th Street. Vivacious and pretty, with an attractive voice that easily carried the tunes of the day, Katie had a large circle of friends, but was especially attracted by Al, whom she had met in 1894. Their acquaintance ripened despite the opposition of her family, who were reluctant to have her linked to a man who still had stage ambitions.

Finally, in May 1900, he renounced those ambitions and he and Katie were married. They spent that summer in Bath Beach by the ocean in Brooklyn and then settled down in a flat in Al's old neighborhood, on Madison Street. By the end of 1901 they were the parents of two children; and a life of orderly routine lay before them.

By then, moreover, his political fortunes had begun to improve. Ever since their bolt in 1894, Campbell, Smith and the other recalcitrants in the Seymour Club had been tossing bricks at Patrick Divver with Tom Foley's tacit approval. The time came when Divver had made more enemies than friends. Besides, he was not as careful as he should have been in watching the death and marriage notices, else he would have understood that new people — Jews and Italians and such — were moving into the district. Foley did better in attracting them. With the renewal of attacks from the reformers, led by District Attorney William Travers Jerome, there was widespread talk of a change in leadership. In 1901 Tom Foley, who had never before been eager for the limelight, moved to take over and readily succeeded. Smith was now on the side with power.

His political ambitions were clear, but it was necessary

to move cautiously lest he be accused of thrusting himself forward. His friends often spoke of his services in the campaigns and now and then let the word drop that he would make a fine candidate for the Assembly.

In 1903, when his chance came, he was ready. That was a difficult year for Tammany, with many a fight on its hands and some people thinking it "was in for a grand smash-up." Foley had become impatient with his man in the Assembly. Joseph P. Bourke, who had been elected a little while before, seemed to have forgotten his friends and no longer showed himself in the district. Some fellows were that way; it went to their heads to be up there in Albany and they overlooked the fact that every twelve months another election rolled around.

Foley decided upon a change, and his choice fell upon Smith. "Dig up Al," he told Campbell, "and ready him up." That didn't take much; Al was all set. He had only to send a pal to tell his mother while he dashed off to let Katie know; then he was ready to campaign.

The Democratic nomination was tantamount to election; "it was like rolling off a log," Smith said later. Nevertheless, he played it safe, "took the stump a bit and did a bit of talking." He moved from corner to corner letting the folks hear his oratory, and his young, enthusiastic "voice could be heard a block away in spite of the rattle of the horse cars." After all, he liked that, even apart from the winning.

When the returns were in, Al was jubilant, for he understood that he had come to the opening of a new career. He was still "dead stuck on acting," he told a reporter, "but it's all over now." And if he was "not exactly a star in the house as yet," still he had faith that he would "get the center of the stage and bask in the political limelight" before he was through.

Smith reached Albany for the first time on a grim January evening in 1904. He came into the cheerless railroad station, along with Tom Caughlan of "Battery Dan" Finn's First District. Campbell had, in preparation, taken him down to Brooks Brothers on Astor Place to buy a cutaway and a spike-tail dress suit. But Al was woefully unprepared for all of that. He had rarely before then spent time away from the city of his birth; nor was he accustomed to staying away from home. He was fearful and uneasy as he looked through the doors onto the darkening, strange town.

Caughlan was more experienced and led the way to a second-class hotel on Broadway. Al was to spend a good part of the next few years in such establishments.

Being an assemblyman was at first no fun; in fact, it was actually distressing. Smith had no idea of what the job entailed. Seriously he attended the sessions of the Legislature, but found himself entirely disregarded and completely confused. No one paid him the least attention; he seemed to have no function but to cast his vote regularly as he was directed by the party leaders. Earnestly he made an effort to find out what was going on. But the task seemed hopeless. Each morning a stack of bills was delivered to his desk and his futile efforts to sort them out or to make sense of them were completely frustrating. Lonely, without the companionship of his wife, lacking friends, and uncomfortable in boardinghouse life, he was thoroughly unhappy and "went home without knowing what it was all about." It seemed not to matter, for he was re-elected as a matter of course in 1904 and 1905.

The second session was no better. He made no speeches but found himself on the committees on banking and on forests. Alas, he had been in a bank only once in his life, to serve a jury notice, and he had never seen a forest. He did venture to introduce a number of private bills in behalf of individuals in his district. But nothing came of them and the whole process seemed futile. Again, despite his earnest efforts, he found it difficult to make head or tail of the work of the Legislature. Waving a fistful of bills in Tommy Caughlan's face one day, he exploded. "I can tell a haddock from a hake by the look in its eye," he said, "but in two hundred years I could not tell these things from a bale of hay." When he returned to New York in the summer of 1905 he demanded that Foley find him a new job. He was unhappy; the fifteen-hundred-dollar salary was not adequate to his needs; and he seemed to be getting nowhere.

Foley mollified the younger man by throwing his way some of the real estate business in judicial receiverships. And despite his disgruntlement at the failure to make his mark in the first fruitless sessions, Smith had learned a great deal. Indeed, he had laid the basis for the mastery of the processes of government that would stand him in good stead the rest of his life. He had roomed with young Robert Wagner, a graduate of the City College and of New York Law School, who introduced Al to some of the mysteries of legislation. The duties of an assemblyman between sessions he understood well enough — to be "an active and helpful assistant to his district leader." Now he learned that those duties extended to Albany, that there were ways of obtaining the things the district required if one knew "when and where to go" and "with what individuals" to deal.

In the next two sessions, the scope of his experience widened further. He attracted the attention of James Wadsworth, aristocratic Republican Speaker of the Assembly, who made him a member of the insurance committee charged with the responsibility of recommending legislation in the light of the Hughes investigation of life insurance companies. Another assignment, to the committee on cities, gave him his first great chance to make himself felt in the Assembly. He was able at last to catch a glimpse of some of the hidden wheels that turned the machinery of state.

Already he had learned by experience that the Fourth Ward existed within New York County and that District Leader Foley, powerful as he was at home, had to accommodate himself to the interests of his peers within the Tammany wigwam. Now he saw that the Hall itself was but one element in the Democratic Party; and that other chieftains with their own followings in Brooklyn and the Bronx and in the upstate cities were by no means docilely inclined to accept instruction from the Tammany sachems.

Back home the Republicans had been altogether alien enemies. They were ready, all right, to wrap themselves in the mantle of reform in Manhattan, although everyone knew that the Union Leaguers when they needed help sent down to the old Fifth District, "the home of the original Philadelphia Repeaters." And out-of-town it was even worse. Somehow the ballots up in Broome County were always getting lost or burned just after they swept the G.O.P. candidate into the Executive Mansion. The rural count always was delayed until the Republicans knew how many votes they needed to make up for their deficit in the city.

That was why talk of rustic virtue went down hard. Smith got tired of hearing of the idyllic villages where "everybody knows his neighbor" and nothing can go wrong. On the floor of the Assembly, a member said, "Yes, and they even know the neighbor's horse when he goes down the road," to which Al suggested that "possibly the horse might answer for him on election day if he was away." There was more snickering than surprise on the Democrats' side when Jonathan P. Allds, Republican leader of the Senate, was trapped in bribery in 1909.

In the Legislature, Smith discovered the Republicans were human — they had eyes, ears and hands like other people. He watched James Wadsworth come down from the speaker's rostrum and saw him greeted by his wife who "put her arms around his neck and kissed him." She might have been Katie down on Oliver Street waiting for her man to be through with his job.

As the sessions passed, Al came to know these small-town lawyers and merchants and farmers. He saw them marshaled by their bosses just as he was by his own. They were no less, but no more, corrupt than anyone else. And while they were certainly different, it proved possible to get along with them. As he listened to the fiery orators assail one another in the chamber and then watched the bitterness dissolve in the cloakrooms, as he saw the operators ease a bill through committee by give and take, he came to understand how vital accommodation and compromise were to the business of government in a democracy.

That was the first task of the good leader. No one had

his own way all the time, — not he or Foley or Croker or the Democrats; not Wadsworth or Boss Platt or the Republicans. But reasonable fellows who really knew what their constituents wanted could always get together and work something out.

Smith went back to the session of 1906 a wiser and more effective legislator. In the next four years, as he applied himself to the assemblyman's job, the range of his acquaintanceships broadened. He became known as a man who could be relied upon. When he had first gone up to Albany, Foley had told him, "If you make a promise, keep it; and if you tell anything, tell the truth." Smith adhered to this code, worked hard, and learned fast. He attracted a coterie of friends who met with him for corned beef and cabbage dinners, and soon he had the confidence of a number of people placed in critical positions.

In 1908 Al went down to Long Island and for the first time met the leader of Tammany Hall. Charles F. Murphy was then staying at his estate, Good Ground.

The life of a country gentleman had not come easily to Murphy. He had been born in the gashouse district north of the Fourth Ward in 1858 and had earned local prominence as catcher on a popular sandlot baseball team. Industrious and hard-working, he had saved his salary as a driver on the carlines and opened a saloon on Nineteenth Street at Avenue A. The Sylvan Social Club that met there quickly acquired power; and by 1890 Murphy owned four saloons.

Later he became heavily involved in contracts, municipal and private. John J. "Brother Jack" Murphy and James "Twin" Gaffney formed a remarkably successful firm that controlled valuable pier facilities and showed a startling knack at persuading railroads and utilities of its excellence in contracting. By the time Smith met him, Murphy was in process of accumulating the two million dollars he would leave at his death.

Silent Charlie had taken over the leadership of Tammany Hall in 1902 after an interregnum created when Croker fled in the face of new revelations of corruption. Murphy then entered upon fifteen years of intermittent guerrilla warfare to consolidate his power. Attacked from behind by ambitious rivals, assaulted by Republicans on one flank and by assorted reformers on the other, he clung on tenaciously and finally won. But he could not hold out without some steps toward rehabilitating the Hall. He gave orders that the police department be cleaned up, made peace with the other borough leaders, and began to think of bringing new men into the forefront.

It early occurred to him that the attractive assemblyman from the Fourth Ward might go far. Soon Smith and Murphy drew closer. They met regularly for luncheon conferences at Delmonico's or saw each other out at Canoe Place Inn. There were other indications also that Al was being singled out for distinction. Ever since Charles Evans Hughes's insurance investigation had shown the need for reform, Tammany had supported stricter regulation. Smith, already a member of the insurance committee, took a prominent part in the enactment of the new statutes.

By now he was learning to distinguish among the multitude of bills that dropped upon his desk. A phenomenal memory stood him in good service. Gradually he came to understand that amidst the mass of proposed legislation only a few measures were actually important. He studied the appropriations bills with care and realized that these were the heart of the State's control. By 1910, few of his colleagues understood as well as he the mysteries of state government.

Slowly too he began to comprehend the connections between the legislator and the people he represented. Coming back to Oliver Street, he would hear the men talk about what bothered them. Or Foley would tell him what the district needed. It was Smith's job to try to deliver.

Significantly, his first speech in the Assembly was a defense of his native city's right to more equitable representation. Thereafter Al introduced a succession of bills in the interest of his constituents. He favored laws to regulate the sale of narcotics, to legalize Sunday baseball, and to repeal the Sunday restrictions on saloons. By 1908, the reform-minded Citizens' Union was judging him "increasingly active and aggressive; very much above average in intelligence, force, and usefulness, though still inclined to follow the machine in support of bad measures."

The disapproval expressed in the last phrase was not important to Smith. The machine was not something apart, but an integral element of city life. This was the mechanism through which politics functioned. The politician, like the actor, expressed the thoughts and emotions of those who were his audience. To do so he had to keep in close touch with his constituency; and the machine was his instrument for doing so.

Seven years of apprenticeship had given Al Smith the mastery of his trade of politics. He knew how the wheels turned in the state government and what made them turn. He understood why some bills passed and others failed —

and in whose interests. But he had still to learn how to put this knowledge to use.

Thus far loyalty to the group which gave him power and the interests of his constituents were his only guides. If the upstaters attempted to encroach upon the privileges of the city, he resisted. Again and again he argued that New York was not adequately represented in the Legislature; the apportionment set by the constitution of 1894 deliberately discriminated against it. Out of municipal pride, also, he tried to limit membership on the transit commission to local residents. Then too, he knew that the people who had voted for him were anxious to have ferry fares and pawnbrokerage rates of interest lowered. It was in their interest to regulate the sale of ice and fish, to ease the tasks of the Salvation Army, and to control the manufacture of cocaine and of cigarettes. Smith likewise was aware that politically active groups like the members of the militia, the veterans, policemen, firemen, wardens and teachers had influence; and he frequently supported measures in their behalf. Nor did it hurt to propose that Columbus day be made a holiday, when the number of Italian voters was increasing.

Since he thus acted on behalf of those who had elected him, Al often thought of himself as the champion of the people against "the interests" — the public utility corporations and the ice and coal companies upon whom every urban resident was dependent. There was not a man or woman in the district who did not feel the pinch of paying for these essential goods and services; and there was no better way to popularity than to bring the costs down. As assemblyman, Smith introduced or voted for bills to lower gas and telephone charges, to regulate the rates, the officers' salaries, and the pooling practices of insurance companies, to control savings banks more rigidly and to tax advertising posters.

In these matters, he acted in terms of no general social theory; he simply defended his side against the opposition — us against them. That did not, of course, stand in the way of occasional accommodations, as in 1909 when he supported the "New York Central grab" arranged by Senator Grady, the Democratic leader of the upper house. There was no contradiction. The various sides arrayed in conflict were not totally opposed to one another. They had no intention of battling one another to the death. Rather, they struggled for the advantageous accommodations which were the life of politics.

As yet, Smith did not understand that some men throughout the country were raising a broader issue. In both houses of the Congress, for instance, bands of determined insurgents were also attacking the interests. Some of them had taken their lead from Theodore Roosevelt; others had gone beyond the former President. Such men had their counterparts in the states, as in La Follette's Wisconsin, and in the cities, as in Golden-Rule Jones's Toledo or Tom Johnson's Cleveland. To them the interests were not merely an opposition to be bargained with but, rather, sinister obstacles in the way of progress. Fired by the dream of human improvement through ever more efficient production, the progressives considered the selfish and corrupting efforts of men of wealth to control the economic and the political order a social danger. To meet the threat it was essential to turn government into an effective instrument of progress by purifying and strengthening it. The battle, from their perspective, was one of principle — of good against evil, of the future against the dead hand of the past.

Smith, whose mind operated through the grasp of concrete facts, had no comprehension whatever of the vague, abstract, and ill-defined philosophy of the progressives. The mavericks and reformers who uttered these fine phrases seemed not really to know what they were talking about. Their politics was not the politics of actuality, and consequently they were often unpredictable and eccentric.

Furthermore, Al and his friends were troubled by the queer company the progressives kept. Sometimes they joined forces with the municipal reformers, "a lot of carpetbaggers" who "get themselves into the limelight by knocking Tammany." At other times, the progressives associated with men who voiced strange and disorderly ideas. In their reforming zeal, they threatened to upset family life and religion and all established social relationships.

Their influence had already made trouble in both political parties. Among the Republicans, Charles Evans Hughes had gone on from the exposure of the insurance interests to challenge the recognized party leadership. Tammany had occasionally supported the measures he proposed as governor. But he did not play the game, and was a danger until he was shunted off into the Supreme Court.

Similar characters, alas, were intruding in the Democratic Party. For illustrations of the danger, the regulars had only to recall their troubles with William Randolph Hearst. There was a rich young man whose wealth and newspapers gave him power enough. But he wanted more; and in his raids on politics he wielded the weapons of reform with such energy that it was hard to tell where sincerity ended and self-interest began. Tom Foley never for a moment trusted him; for Smith that was reason enough to oppose the publisher's grab for the mayoralty in 1905. A year later Tammany gave Hearst the gubernatorial nomination — "the dirtiest day's work of my career," said Tom Grady. The result had been a Republican victory. Yet Hearst remained ambitious and showed no sign of gratitude toward the party. The audacity of such freebooters proved it was time to call a halt to the drift toward progressivism. Fortunately, as one of the boys put it, "They ain't no Democratic votes on Fifth Avenue. They're over on Ninth and Tenth Avenues where I live."

The issue was drawn in the legislative session of 1910 when Hughes proposed an extensive list of reforms including the direct primary and measures strengthening the state public service commissions. Smith and the other Tammany men went down the line to defeat the Governor. In the same way, they supported the Republican regulars when the insurgents in the G.O.P. opposed the choice of J. P. Allds as president of the Senate.

As a result the Citizens' Union, though recognizing his ability, criticized Smith and Robert Wagner, his colleague in the Senate, and called for their defeat. But such pinpricks did not disturb a veteran politician.

Smith was by now established. His family had grown with the addition of three more children between 1904 and 1909. He felt secure; and although his fame did not as yet run much beyond the boundaries of his own district, he was nonetheless a person of status. It was a sign of his arrival in 1904 when he became a member of the Friendly Sons of St. Patrick. In the same year he had moved to a better flat on Peck Slip, and in 1907 to a half-house on Oliver Street, where he remained for the next fourteen years. He had come a long way from the Fulton Fish Market; and his course was set toward a career of loyalty and steady advancement within the organization.

I I I

Approaches to Leadership

A WAVE OF DISCONTENT, sweeping across the nation in 1910, brought disruptive groups of progressives to power in many places. Dissatisfaction with the Taft administration and with Republican conservative leadership elected a Democratic Congress. In New Jersey Woodrow Wilson, a college president, became governor. And New York State, for the first time in two decades, fell completely into the hands of the Democrats. The new force that thus achieved prominence cut across the usual party battles and indirectly altered the line of Smith's career.

Few Republicans were able to assess the character of the overturn correctly. In Democratic eyes the election of 1910 was simply the opportunity for a return to the rewards of office. Not for many years had the party controlled the governorship and both houses of the Legislature.

The New York County leaders were determined to make the most of their opportunities. But they knew also that they would have to be circumspect in their dealings. They were hardly in a position to forget that their power in the state depended upon alliances with other Democrats in Brooklyn and in the upstate cities. Governor John Dix himself was not one of their men, but the candidate of the progressive Democratic League. In his inaugural address he had given notice that his would be a "businessman's" administration, distinguished by economy and "giving to the public dollar the same purchasing power as the private dollar." What was more, sprinkled throughout the party's ranks were influential reformers who had in the past shown a distressing inclination to go their own way if their sensibilities were offended. These folk would have to be appeased.

The Tammany chieftains, of course, had no intention of surrendering techniques, tried and tested, within their districts. When Al turned up at the August outings he saw the same masses of children about the merry-go-round, the freely-flowing beer for the adults, the excited dancing late on into the night, the sleepy boatride back, and the final exhilaration of the torchlit parade on the way home from the pier. On Christmas Day, "Sarsaparilla" Riley still stood at the head of the stairs in 207 Bowery ready to exclude the goats from among the seven thousand guests who turned up for dinner. On his mother's birthday, Big Tim Sullivan still gave away two thousand pairs of shoes in an annual display of generosity.

But Murphy and his advisers dimly understood that more than that would be needed under the new conditions. Eager to put Tammany's best foot forward, they were willing to compromise when some of the independent Democrats objected that the old-timers, blessed with seniority but scarred by past battles, ought not to take command of the Legislature. The organization thus acquiesced in the election of Daniel D Frisbie of Schoharie as Speaker of the Assembly; and it looked to its own young members to take up the other important legislative places. Times were changing, and it would no longer do to have the old characters in the foreground.

There was "Paradise Jimmy" Oliver, for instance, from the old Fourth Ward, who had been minority leader of the Assembly in 1907. Jimmy had a heart of gold. Everyone knew the story. Years and years ago he had been a baker on the Bowery and had, now and then, slipped a hot roll to a shivering newsboy who grew up to be Big Tim Sullivan and helped his benefactor on in politics. And Oliver had ability; Big Tim "wouldn't have backed a 'dead one' even with the hot rolls in mind." Paradise Jimmy was a handy man with his fists and few were his equal at setting the boys at the bar to laughing or at spreading good humor through an audience.

These, however, no longer seemed the talents appropriate to leadership in the Assembly. Too many people remembered that Oliver had long been known as a gamblers' attorney, and his colleagues were more than likely to laugh at, instead of with, him. He bought a Prince Albert and a silk topper. But as the "Beau Brummell of the Bowery" he remained a fair mark for the sneers of the legislators. Every now and then, in the excitement of debate, the habits of the street would trip him up in speech or behavior and the point he wished to make would be lost in ridicule. And then, sometimes he took a drop too many. Such a man, though he did not regularly associate with bishops and bankers, nevertheless had a dignity of his own. But "the reform gang" did not recognize it and it was hopeless now to think of him in a place of responsibility.

It was better to depend on a younger man who was loyal

and yet who commanded the respect of the Assembly. Al Smith had proved himself on both counts; he knew his place in the organization and he had demonstrated his ability in the chamber. There was general approval when he was designated majority leader of the Assembly when the session of 1911 opened. For much the same reasons, Tammany allowed the Senate to pass over the claims of the veteran Thomas F. Grady and to choose young Robert Wagner as its temporary president and majority leader.

The reformers continued to make trouble, however. On January 15, 1911, Al Smith had stood with big Tom Foley in the lobby of the Hotel Ten Eyck in Albany, their cigars tilting upward at the ceiling. Through the doors of the restaurant they could see Murphy at dinner with the bosses of Buffalo and Erie County. Now and then a lesser chieftain joined them for consultation. The decision was being shaped that would designate a United States Senator at the party caucus the next day. In time the word came. It was to be Blue-eyed Billy Sheehan of Buffalo.

A small group of independents refused to go along. Twenty-five of the one hundred and fifteen Democrats had absented themselves from the caucus and were not bound by its decision. Mostly first-year men, elected in normally Republican districts, they kept "a sharp eye out" for "the sentiment of the folk back home." Joining the Republicans, they blocked any action for almost three months, and kept the legislature in endless confusion through much of the session. And it was all for nothing; from the point of view of the regulars, the dissidents never knew what they were doing.

Prominent among them was Franklin D. Roosevelt, a

young senator serving his first term from Dutchess County. This college boy, whose distinguished name carried weight in the headlines, thought himself a Galahad battling corruption while all the time he was only boxing with shadows.

Now, everyone knew that Sheehan had had a long career in politics and the hypercritical could dig around for this or that incident in his record. But it all amounted to little; and it was rank hypocrisy to accuse him of representing Thomas Fortune Ryan and the traction interests. When you got right down to it, in what did he differ from the insurgents' candidate, T. R. Shepard, who was an attorney for the Pennsylvania Railroad and had originally been supported by Boss McCooey of Brooklyn? Sheehan was an Irish Catholic who had always been a straight machine man, while Shepard was a Protestant Yankee, a member of respectable clubs and an author, but a man who had veered with every whim from affiliation to affiliation. It almost seemed as if a surface gentility were to be the test of fitness for the senatorial toga. Behind the whole struggle, it was rumored, was the influence of Francis Lynde Stetson, counsel for J. P. Morgan; and few reformers understood in whose interests they really acted.

In the end, of course, no one gained from the turmoil. Sheehan lost his chance; but so did Shepard. Murphy perhaps fared best of all. O'Gorman, who finally was selected, was more his man than Sheehan had been; and in addition the Tammany leader was able to move his son-in-law, Daniel F. Cohalan, to the judge's bench vacated by O'Gorman. Murphy watched with relief and perhaps with cynical amusement as the tired reformers went down the line in the vote for O'Gorman and Cohalan.

Smith had not taken a leading role in the struggle, although he loyally supported the party caucus. But he was chairman of the Committee on Ways and Means and member of the Committee on Rules; and through the months that followed he found himself increasingly drawn into conflict with the insurgents who continued to make pests of themselves. "Playing to the galleries," they showed a maddening tendency in the next four years to let vague principles sweep the realities of the situation out of sight.

For them, the bill to separate the Bronx from New York County somehow involved democracy and self-determination; Smith saw in it a grab for power by a none too honest politician, supported by Republicans anxious to weaken Tammany. The insurgents were unhappy when "ripper bills" legislated entrenched Republicans out of office to make room for deserving Democrats. To Al this was merely "recovering stolen goods." Protracted negotiations in 1911 produced a new charter, not ideal perhaps, but one that satisfied the city's desire for home rule, the scruples of reform Mayor Gaynor, the interests of the traction companies, and the tactical needs of Tammany. Yet the Municipal Research Bureau charged that the document "literally invites plunder and chloroforms the victim"; and it took inordinate persuasion to get independent legislators like Roosevelt to vote for it.

The critical issue of the reapportionment of congressional districts involved the same tug at the conscience of the reformers by abstract ideals on the one hand and by practical considerations on the other. It was one thing to agree to an equitable redistribution of seats and another to find one's own county the loser. No such scruples troubled Tammany, which had but one criterion, its own power. Nor did any sense of "false delicacy" restrain Murphy's men from using "clubs or axes if necessary" to secure the passage of the kind of election law they desired in 1911. The same realism determined Tammany's attitude toward the direct primary. The machine had fought the idea for years; but when it became apparent that resistance would no longer be effective, it accepted the inevitable and labored to get as advantageous a law as possible. "Within four hours I've become an advocate of direct primaries," said Al Smith. "Maybe I did so because I had to. But, never mind, I did so."

To Smith and his friends, the mechanism of government was less important than the men at the controls. Just as they accepted the direct primary and learned to use it toward their own ends, so they knew that a civil service commission was only what a governor made it. Personal relationships alone counted. "If it comes to the point where I've got to break my word to the fellows I'm working with here each day," Al once said, "I'm willing to quit this legislative game."

This the reformers did not understand in putting their principles before loyalty. Their dissent weakened the party. In 1911 the legislative program had all but collapsed in the long struggle over the senatorship; and internal divisions thereafter sometimes made it easier for Smith and Wagner to work with the Republicans than with their own party. Governor Dix was confused, torn between the machine and the insurgents. Whatever useful ideas he had, as for the development of water power, were lost in the disorder.

The old-timers like Big Tim Sullivan were sure that *reform, there ain't nothin' to it.* Yet in the off-year election in November 1911, the Democrats lost their majority in the Assembly; and a Republican-dominated fusion administration took control of the municipal government. Furthermore, there were serious threats to the position of Tammany in the party. The Governor wavered among the several factions, so that patronage was no longer an effective means of discipline. Murphy found it a struggle to keep a grip on the state committee and he had frequent cause to be grateful for Al's services.

In the summer of 1912, the Tammany men discovered the full extent of their difficulties at the national convention in Baltimore, where they encountered William Jennings Bryan, once the boy orator, and three times candidate for the presidency.

The "peerless loser," as he was known in New York, could hardly in good conscience ask for the nomination once more. But he had every intention of dictating the choice and finding a strategic place in the new administration. A man of enormous sincerity, he floated along in a cloud of self-righteousness that kept him out of contact with reality. Since he never had doubts as to either his own virtue or wisdom, he was able to take almost any position with utter conviction. For years he had led his wild agrarian following along to the tune of free silver. Now the farmers, grown fat with relative prosperity, had discovered they were after all respectable property owners and had lost interest in radicalism. Was it not fortunate then that Bryan had made a discovery of his own — that the source of all evils in the party and the nation was Tammany, which, in a corrupt alliance with the financiers like Thomas Fortune Ryan, threatened to conquer the nation? The new tune evoked the countryman's dislike of the city, and carried with it spine-tingling overtones of xenophobia and anti-Catholicism.

This was a puzzler for the New Yorkers. Why should anyone buy this shoddy line? Any Bowery boy knew enough to sniff twice when too much corned beef and cabbage was offered for a nickel. But then, alas, the hinterland was full of hicks — the purchasers of gold bricks, avaricious for an easy way to turn a fast dollar or to find a quick answer. Their speculative mania kept them and everyone else in trouble. Ready to run crying justice to the government when they found the satchel stuffed with old newspapers, they never considered that it was their own foolhardy avarice, their own assumption of superiority over the stranger, that made the deal in the first place.

Now Tammany was the target of their wrath and would remain so for two decades. Antagonism to the New Yorkers was the cement that bound the Bryanite agrarians to the Wilsonite reformers. Together they controlled the convention.

Murphy and his followers yielded. They went along with the ticket. But even victory in November did not end the uneasiness with which they viewed their future in the party.

In the three-way battle with Theodore Roosevelt's Progressives and the Taft Republicans the Democrats readily won out. The voters who made Wilson President also elected strong Democratic majorities in both houses of the Legislature and a Democratic governor in New York State.

By 1912 the Democrats had had enough of John Dix, who in the attempt to please every faction had lost the favor of all. The Governor himself was tired of the constant

trading of patronage for support and was not really eager
to run again. Maneuvering for a place on the national
ticket, he alienated the independents, organized as the
Empire State Democracy. Tammany, impatient with him,
but lacking a candidate of its own and fearful of what the
New York Wilsonites might do, finally gave its reluctant
support to Congressman William Sulzer, a man who for
the moment seemed co-operative yet had reform support.

Sulzer was a bizarre character, vain, self-important, and
stupid. At the state convention, "trying to seem a good
mixer — in a silk hat and long coat," he had built a boom
for himself and never realized that he had been selected as
a nonentity with few enemies. "Bashful Bill" had no personal following. Yet the two votes for the presidential
nomination thrown to him in Baltimore went to his head.
Once in office, he was deceived by ambition in the belief
that he could build a machine of his own by catering to the
reform crowd. He was soon at loggerheads with the Democrats in the Legislature as well as with the party organization.

It was not long before he was undeceived. Murphy was
disgusted with the Governor's hypocrisy. The man had
"fed at the public crib himself for twenty-three years.
What right" had he "to complain now?" Besides, Murphy
by now was impatient of these freebooters. He could look
across the river at the horrible example of New Jersey,
where Woodrow Wilson had pulled himself to power by
disrupting the party machine; and the Tammany leader
had no intention of allowing Sulzer to use him in the
same fashion. The Legislature was ordered to destroy the
Governor. "Bashful Bill" never knew what hit him. Once
his bluff was called he could only keep raising the stakes
in the hope of postponing the day of reckoning.

With the return of the Democrats to power, Al Smith became Speaker of the Assembly. It was his job to lead the attack. After a period of guerrilla warfare during which Sulzer withheld patronage and flirted with Hearst while the Legislature disregarded his program, the decision was made to get rid of him. Smith had not been eager for the battle; he disliked "going to the bat blind," without a clear view of the consequences. But as Speaker he had to take the first step, presentation by the Assembly of articles of impeachment against Sulzer. The charge against the Governor, that he had misspent campaign funds, was well-founded. But little would have been made of it had he not antagonized the machine. Smith had no illusions, in the weeks of bitter debate in 1913, as to what the issue was. The Governor had proved a traitor and had put his own interests above those of the party. That was enough for those who were loyal to the organization. He was "worse than an anarchist," more "dangerous than the man who gets up on the street and waves the red flag," Al declaimed. In due course, the impeachment was carried in the Assembly and the Governor found guilty in the Senate.

The removal of Sulzer did not end Tammany's difficulties. In 1913, another off-year, the Democratic mayoralty candidate was beaten by the reformer John Purroy Mitchel. At the same time, Tammany again lost control of the Assembly and Smith moved down to the position of minority leader. He, along with everyone else, was conscious that 1914 would see the election of a new governor.

Murphy remained in hot water. A coalition seemed to be forming to oust him from the leadership. Sulzer's successor, Lieutenant-Governor Martin H. Glynn, maneuvered cautiously to pick up as much personal support as possible. From Washington, Wilson's administration, through Dudley Field Malone, Collector of the Port, supported various anti-Tammany groups. With the municipal administration in the hands of Mitchel, all the sources of patronage had dried up. Meanwhile, a number of free-wheeling reformers, through ambition or persistence, kept up a barrage of criticism and a crusading district attorney hounded Murphy's friends. Justice Dan Cohalan was attacked on a bribery charge. "Curly Joe" Cassidy, Democratic boss of Queens, was convicted of selling judgeships, and State Treasurer Kennedy committed suicide while under investigation. There were new revelations of graft in the police department. Then, in January 1914, rumors emanating from administration sources in Washington suggested that Murphy's enemy, Franklin Roosevelt, might run for governor. In February the reform Democrats made the celebration of the Tilden Centennial the occasion for bitter attacks upon Tammany. At the same time Murphy faced an assault on another front from old Tammany men he had earlier ousted, Bourke Cockran and Boss Croker.

There was trouble even on the East Side. Sulzer had come down to Madison Street in the election of 1913 to try to defeat Smith. His appearance there had made a Donnybrook Fair seem like a Quaker meeting; "every time you see a head, hit it." Nobody worried about the oratory; the horse cars, which somehow had stepped up their schedules from half-hour to two-minute intervals, drowned the former governor out. But there were all sorts of Italians, Jews, and other new people in the district and Foley was taking no chances. He insisted that Murphy get rid of Mike Rofrano and State Senator James Frawley, whose sinister intentions he suspected. In this free-for-all

atmosphere, anything could happen. The man who failed
to keep his guard up was lost.

Of that fault, Murphy rarely was guilty. Warily he
watched his opponents for the lead that would permit him
to bring them down. In February, when his fortunes were
at their lowest ebb, Judge Edward F. O'Dwyer gave him
the opportunity. All the Tammany chiefs were members
of the National Democratic Club. O'Dwyer learned that
some of them, through oversight, had forgotten to pay
their dues on time. On his motion, Murphy and Foley
were thrown out in a bold but incautious effort to dis-
credit them. He seemed to have the approval of the
national administration and of Glynn in this first step
to unseat the county leader.

But he reckoned without Murphy's agility. Murphy
understood that control of the party machinery was more
important to him than control of the government. The
word went out to the Tammany men in Congress and in
the Assembly to close ranks. Suddenly Wilson and Glynn
found their legislative programs threatened by the defection of crucial votes. The President was particularly hard-
pressed, for he needed those votes to enact the Panama
Tolls Repeal Act, close to his heart.

The opposition collapsed. Glynn began to put patronage
in Tammany's way. Malone broke with him, and Wilson
disassociated himself from the conflict. In April, Murphy
was triumphantly reinstated in the club, and in the scurry
to placate him, O'Dwyer was unceremoniously abandoned.
In June, in a final triumph, Tammany discovered it could
use the direct primary more effectively than its foes. Ad-
hering to the letter of the law, Smith on Murphy's behalf
got the party convention to refrain from designating pri-

mary candidates. Names would appear on the ballot only
through petition; and the machine was far more effective
in collecting signatures than the reformers.

The battle was over, although desultory sniping con-
tinued. During the summer Franklin Roosevelt still im-
agined he might secure the senatorial nomination, and in
September he still ventured to attack James W. Gerard,
Murphy's choice. A month later he had to eat his words.
In the winter, the insurgents made some efforts to seize the
federal patronage, but O'Gorman frustrated them in the
Senate.

The bitterness of this guerrilla warfare carried over
into the election of 1914. With the Democrats divided,
the Progressives still in the field, and Sulzer running on
his own American Party, the Republicans carried the
mayoralty, the governorship and both houses of the Legislature. More certainly than ever before they were in a
position to recast the state government in their own interest. The constitutional convention due to meet the
year following was to be the means to that end.

Through the years of attack and counterattack between
1910 and 1914, Al had served valiantly and loyally in
Murphy's army. The prominence of his role confirmed
the impression, in progressive circles, that Smith, though
powerful and able, was but a reactionary party hack. After
all, he had defended the race tracks and boxing. He had
ridiculed the idea of sending policemen to college and had
helped defeat the woman's suffrage bill. And of the district
primary he had said, "This sort of thing is only the squawk
of the fellows on the outs, the squawk which, like Niagara
Falls, runs on forever." There had been some talk of

running him for the presidency of the Borough of Manhattan or of the Board of Aldermen in 1913. But even Tammany then thought it unwise to risk putting him on the ballot for a general office.

Yet in the day-to-day business of the Legislature Smith had not found his party loyalty incompatible with the support of measures in the interests of his constituents; and some of those measures had a progressive aspect. He had helped enact laws to regulate private bankers, to protect the purchasers of coal against short weight, and to further conservation. He had aided in the ratification of the federal income tax amendment and had, ultimately, even voted for the direct primary. In all these actions, there had been no commitment to an ideology, but rather a pragmatic judgment of the rights and wrongs as well as of the political utility of each measure. Smith did not yet recognize that there was a general pattern to the specific positions he took.

The basis for that understanding had, however, already been established, in the aftermath of a great disaster, the shock of which compelled many New Yorkers to think seriously about the society developing around them.

At 4:40 P.M. on Saturday, March 25, 1911, fire broke out on the eighth floor of a building on Washington Place. Fortunately the structure was only ten years old and fireproof. The fire did not spread below the floor on which it started and the workers there descended quickly to safety by the elevators and stairs.

The eighth floor and the two above it were occupied by the Triangle Waist Company, an enterprise which sometimes employed as many as a thousand hands. On this day, in the slack season, some six hundred of them were

preparing to go home. Closing time was only five minutes
off. As the flames consumed the bolts of cloth and the
stacked-up boxes of finished goods and burst out through
the windows, the workers on Ten in alarm hastened up
to the roof, clambered across a neighboring building and
got down to the street with the aid of students from the
New York University Law School, next door.

The girls on Nine also heard the alarm. The acrid odor
of singed clothing and the reflected tongues of fire in
the window panes brought danger close to them. They
left the machines and moved hurriedly toward the exit.
As the women nearest it opened the door, however, they
hesitated. They formed a clump that grew steadily in size,
with those behind pushing and those in front drawing
back. Now the realization spread, which they had all the
time known but forgotten, that there was no exit except
down to the eighth floor, where the fire was.

Panic took hold. Some of the girls dashed to the windows
and crowded out onto the narrow cornice. In the face of
the 110-foot drop, they drew back, only to find the way
blocked off by the crowds pushing away from the center
of the loft. Then it became a matter of clinging to some
precarious hold on the ledge. Some were jostled off or,
maddened with despair, surrendered their grip; forty thus
met death on the sidewalks of New York.

Within the ninth floor, the girls milled about in agoniz-
ing indecision. A mass of screaming women surged desperately toward a staircase that led to the roof, only to
discover that it was closed off with an iron latticework gate.
The outer edges of the pool kept spreading as new arrivals
who could not see the gate crowded in. There was a
similar jam at the locked door through the partition sep-

arating the workroom from the elevators. Later the firemen would find a hundred bodies suffocated or trampled
to death. In all, one hundred and forty-three lives were
lost.

News of the Triangle fire horrified the whole city. On
Sunday some one hundred thousand people passed through
the morgue in the effort to identify the victims. The
district attorney called for an investigation. At a mass
funeral on April 5, fully fifty thousand mourners marched
in the rain for five hours, "claiming the seven uniden-
tified dead as their brothers and sisters." A meeting at
the Metropolitan Opera House heard banker Jacob H.
Schiff, Bishop David H. Greer, and Rabbi Stephen S. Wise
call for the relief of those who had suffered and for action
to prevent future holocausts. Shortly, a Committee on
Safety was working to see that it did not happen again.
Its members were among the city's most distinguished
citizens — Henry L. Stimson, George W. Perkins, R. Bayard Cutting, Henry Morgenthau, and Anne Morgan.

It was not, however, easy to locate the blame for the
disaster. The fire had not struck in one of those dingy
sweatshops so often the target of investigators' disapproval,
but in a large, modern, fireproof plant. Nor was it possible
to convict the owners of criminal negligence. They were
found innocent of any violation of the law. Yet the barred
exits had taken one hundred and forty-three lives, and if
there were to be a remedy it was essential to know the
reason.

Some of the speakers at the Opera House had explained
that the tragedy had followed from conditions general to
labor relations in the city. Back in 1909 and 1910, the
Triangle Company had successfully fought off a great

strike of shirtwaist makers. At the time, the girls had complained that the firm made a practice of locking them in to force them to do nightwork when necessary. Many of the strikers had been dismissed to be replaced by more docile hands, most of them recent Italian and Jewish immigrants, and many of them under the age of twenty. Since then, to maintain discipline, to prevent pilfering, and to keep out union organizers, the company had continued to lock all the doors, leaving but one exit on the eighth floor, at which the girls, and the few men who worked with them, could be inspected as they went home.

The deaths in the fire had thus been the end product of an attitude toward labor. "The life of men and women is so cheap and property is so sacred, there are so many of us for one job, it matters little if one hundred and forty-three of us are burned to death," charged Rose Schneiderman of the Women's Trade Union League at the Opera House. The issue thus stated involved not merely fire prevention, but the place of labor in society.

Agitation by the Committee on Safety in June led the Legislature to create a commission to investigate the need for more effective fire prevention, but with a mandate broad enough to include the general problems of labor relations in the state. The commission was to consist of two senators, three assemblymen, and four private citizens. Al Smith helped set up the commission and became one of its members. He was now drawn into the study of a problem with which he had always lived, but which he had not theretofore understood.

For four years the commission dealt with concrete evidence, with facts. There were available to it data on the victims of the fire and on the injured survivors. Case Number 210 was an Italian girl of eighteen, the sole support of her parents. Case Number 120, age thirty, left a wife and two children who had arrived in the United States only three months before and were completely helpless. Case Number 85, a widow of thirty-three, had had dependent upon her five little children, a brother of sixteen, and her aged father and mother. No one was obligated to support those left helpless by injury or death.

The investigators could not but notice the harsh conditions under which men and women worked, even those who escaped disaster — the long hours, the low wages, the fear of the absolute power of the boss. Traveling through the state, visiting every manufacturing town, and missing not a session, Smith began to perceive the helplessness in the industrial order of his own kind of people, not in Manhattan alone, but upstate as well. And he began to understand also that they needed more than an occasional pair of shoes from Big Tim Sullivan.

He was assisted toward that understanding by a deepening acquaintanceship with a type of person he had hardly known before. Dr. Henry Moskowitz, who had spoken on fire protection at the mass meeting, was a member of the Ethical Culture Society and, moved by its social ideals, worked in the Madison Street settlement. Frances Perkins had been secretary of the Committee on Safety. Abram Elkus, counsel of the commission, had also been born on the East Side and was now vice-president of Stephen S. Wise's liberal Free Synagogue. His partner, Joseph M. Proskauer, was active in the Citizens' Union and also in the Educational Alliance on the East Side. Belle Israels, who later married Dr. Moskowitz, was a graduate of Teachers College, and had been on the staff of the Educational Alliance. Mary E. Dreier, a member of the commission, had long labored to improve the condition of working women.

These were reformers, but not the dudes who parted their name in the middle whom Al had known in the Legislature. The members of the commission were interested in politics, and some of them had actually supported the Progressive Party in 1912. But their desire to do good was not abstract. Rather, it led them down into the streets of the East Side where they gave themselves over unselfishly to the improvement of the needy and the helpless. What were their motives? Smith could not fail to be convinced by their sense of dedication. And as he came to impress them with his own earnestness and ability, they accepted him for what he was. Within the terms of their common objectives, they could work together. Apparently party affiliations were not all-important. On some issues, it was not simply a matter of one side against another.

Smith did not lose faith in American capitalism as a result of exposure to its abuses. By and large he found the owners of factories willing to do what they could for their laborers. But legislation was essential to set standards.

From 1911 onward, Al placed before the Asembly a succession of bills to give the government the positive role of protecting those helpless to protect themselves. These were the years when most reformers were agitated by Sheehan and Sulzer and conservation and the primaries. But the type of man, in his cutaway coat and with "a big long shoelace on his eyeglasses," who rose to worry over the fate of migratory birds and fish did not extend his concern to women and children. Smith and Wagner were not surprised to find in the Auburn factory of Thomas Mott Osborne, leader of the Progressive Democrats, "the vilest and most uncivilized conditions of labor in the state." The substantial achievements of the four years after 1911 were made without help from Tammany's enemies.

The fire danger received immediate attention, in measures to establish a Bureau of Fire Prevention and to assure adequate exits, fire drills, fireproofing and automatic sprinklers in factories. Other laws forbade smoking and the use of unprotected gas jets in manufacturing establishments. But already in 1912 there was a wider scope to the proposals Smith supported. That year he helped enact regulations for the ventilation of factories, for the examination of the physical fitness of working children, and for limiting the employment of women after childbirth. There followed in time bills to improve cleanliness and to supply washing facilities and lunchrooms, bills to license bakeries and to register all factories, bills to compel employers to supply female laborers with rest periods and with seats with backs. These laws dealt with petty details but with such as affected the working lives of thousands of men and women.

More general enactments limited the hours of labor of women and children and created a Bureau of Employment in the Department of Labor. Vigilantly Smith frustrated every effort to make exceptions. He had nowhere read in the Bible, he observed on one such occasion, "Remember the Sabbath to keep it holy — except in canneries." So too he fought resourcefully and intelligently for the workmen's compensation law. Enacted in 1911, that measure was struck down by the courts, and finally

in 1913 was put into effect by a constitutional amendment.
Thereafter, however, it was still necessary to protect it
against crippling modifications.

By 1915 Smith had acquired a twofold reputation, as
a machine regular and as a "strong supporter of desirable
industrial and social legislation." This puzzled people who
could not understand that the two roles were quite com-
patible. In that year, Al found a new platform on which
to play them both in the convention that met to revise
the Constitution of the state.

In the convention, Smith found himself in a distinct
minority: the Democrats held only 32 seats as against the
133 of the Republicans. Representing the G.O.P. were
such famous lawyers and proved public servants as Elihu
Root, Henry L. Stimson, Louis Marshall, James Wadsworth, George W. Wickersham, Seth Low, and John Lord
O'Brian. Yet amid this impressive array of legal talent
Smith distinguished himself. He was unsurpassed in his
command of the processes of government and in his understanding of the problems of politics. Able to get to es-
sentials — all the rest was simply mayonnaise poured over
the salad — he made his position clear in vigorous and
forceful speeches studded with concrete illustrations and
East Side metaphors. Many a conservative Republican
concluded with George W. Wickersham that Al had been
"the most useful man in the convention" — of all the participants "the best informed on the business of the State,"
according to Elihu Root. The uptown lawyers went away
with a new conception of what the machine politician
could do.

The convention itself accomplished little. The best
that could be said for the document it produced was

"that it ain't no worse than what was done to us twenty years ago." Ultimately the voters in their wisdom rejected it. But the debate gave Smith an opportunity to review what he had learned in the past five years, and to do so before a wide public.

He was eloquent, for example, in maintaining the power of the state to protect labor and to regulate manufacturing. He defended the minimum wage law for women and children. Battling for workmen's compensation, he portrayed "the utter helplessness" that went with poverty and begged the convention not to reduce the Constitution "to the same level as the caveman's law, the law of the sharpest tooth, the angriest brow and the greediest maw." This was but an indirect tax to help carry the burden of the men injured "in the upbuilding of an industry." There was no paternalism in such measures any more than, say, in aid to a widowed mother for the support of her children. Such enactments were not privileges but acts of self-protection for the general good of the state.

The insistence upon cutting through the *whereases* and the verbiage was characteristic of his realism in the face of all the problems of the convention. Conservation meant more than the protection of a few beauty spots; it meant also "a check upon the greed of men" who "looked for too many crops from their land." The state was not "green fields and rivers and lakes and mountains and cities." Not at all. It was the people. And law was not "the expression of some divine or eternal right," but of "what fits the present-day needs of society, what goes the farthest to do the greatest good for the greatest number."

Al was tough as well as realistic when it came to the rights of his native city. A fraudulent "home rule" proposal gave New Yorkers less freedom to govern themselves than Washington had just given "the Philippines, a half-civilized bunch of half-dressed men that we got by accident." The apportionment of legislative seats discriminated against the metropolis, and the rigid election laws that applied in New York City did not apply upstate.

Ah, he knew all the excuses. The city was just a little corner in a great big imperial state. It was just a commercial point, a seaport settlement. And then there was "the more delicate reason." After all, those new citizens, those new voters didn't understand the government, the institutions, the needs, the traditions of the state. "What do you think of that? The man who comes from a farm, after battling with the handles of the plow, I suppose knows all about it."

The good humor faded as Smith attacked the "ironclad nerve" and the "galvanized gall" of the Republicans. There were some people, of course, for whom the old neighborhoods were not good enough, who fled to the suburbs where they could have "hot and cold folding doors." But, he pointed out, the masses remained where they were, and he asked those who "live two men to a house" to try to understand the problems of their fellow citizens who lived forty to a house.

For himself, he had faith in the equal Americanism of them all. Therefore he kept in close contact with his district and, yes, with Tammany, which was the instrument through which his constituents communicated with their government. That was also why he ventured to suggest that the legislative debates be printed as "a kind of automatic valve on the hot air, and if there is anything needed in this room, it is said valve." It was essential that the people be trusted with democracy. Why, once there was a Socialist from Schenectady in the Assembly "and when he found that the debate was open, free and unrestricted and he was enabled to participate absolutely freely" and "he found that 76 votes and 76 only did anything in this chamber, he went immediately down to the Ten Eyck barbershop and got a haircut."

It was hard to take umbrage with a man who knew the machinery of government as intimately and precisely as did Smith. Fifteen years of experience had given him a comprehension, shared by few of his colleagues, that the forms set forth in the Constitution and in the statutes were not identical with the actuality of practice. The Legislature made the laws with so many readings after so many days; but Smith knew that the governor could use emergency messages to jam his own enactments through. And everyone knew that important bills waited until the end of the session, "and finally in the last days, while the flags are flying from the Capitol and the band is playing and everybody feels happy over the prospect of the last $250 draw and a good time for the summer — they will patch up their differences and say, 'Well, go downstairs and get a message and put it right through' and they do it." Appropriations bills originated in the Assembly; but Smith knew that a small committee really held the power. Department heads prepared budget estimates; but Smith knew which clerks did the work. Under certain circumstances, impeachment proceedings had to wait for a summons from the governor. "What a proclamation that would be . . . Pursuant to the powers vested in me by section and article so-and-so of the Constitution, I hereby convene the Assembly in extraordinary session for the purpose of preparing articles of impeachment against myself."

It made sense to discard the empty forms. Behind the titles were men; and what was important was that the job get done. It was pointless to hedge positions about with legal limitations, to divide power so that no one really could act, to tie the hands of the legislature with minute constitutional prescriptions. It was far more reasonable to give an official a job to do and hold him responsible for it. It was necessary to reorganize the state departments and, through an executive budget, to locate the central responsibility where it belonged, in the governor. Only thus would it be possible to reform fiscal policy and achieve genuine efficiency in government.

Curiously, Smith had arrived, by another road, at the same conclusion as the progressives. For years the reform journals and research reports, in the quest for efficiency and in the eagerness to eliminate corruption, had advocated the reorganization of government along business lines. Smith was no reader of these earnest documents; they were all the same to him. But whenever they had a good idea, he was "more than willing to give them a lift." Some of the progressives he met in the course of the Factory Commission investigation influenced him more. Yet in the last analysis it was through the lessons of his own experience that he came to speak from the same platform as they at the constitutional convention.

The last five years had taught him how crucial was the role of the governor in state affairs. Almost all the political turmoil of the period had originated in that office. The chief executive commanded the enormously powerful weapon of patronage and exercised weighty influence over legislation. Yet none of the men who held the place had succeeded at it.

In part they had been trapped by ambition. It was only natural. The precedents set by Grover Cleveland and Theodore Roosevelt and Woodrow Wilson were fresh and compelling. The governor of a large state like New York automatically became a presidential possibility; and the glitter of the White House blinded Dix and Sulzer, and even Glynn, to the task at hand in the Executive Mansion. Hence they proved incapable of resisting the contrary pulls of the machine that had elected them and of the independent progressives who might be decisive in a national contest. The great influence of the office in the end had counted for nothing.

Perhaps already Smith allowed himself to speculate that he might himself one day have the opportunity to do better. That made little difference in his life. He was more prosperous and more important than he had been as a rank-and-file assemblyman in 1910. But his home was still the East Side, and every Sunday he still walked across the bridge after Mass to visit his mother in Brooklyn. He was one of Foley's boys who took in the picnics at Sulzer's Harlem River Park, who mixed with the fellows in the corner saloon, and who still loved the shows.

One day at the convention, Mark Eisner came hastily in and asked Smith, who was speaking, to yield. He brought news that Al would receive the Democratic nomination for the position of sheriff of New York County. At that moment, Smith caught a glimpse of the greater stage upon which he would sometime stroll, of the more dramatic role he would play, and of the more important lines he would speak.

I V

The Way Up

THE TAMMANY MEN, ordinarily, were not given to self-pity. They knew the facts of life; and in the running battle of politics they understood that some prizes were simply out of reach.

A man like Smith realized that his prospects were extremely narrow. True, there were places of profit and power in local government; and a career in the Assembly or the Senate might lead to the post of party leader. That was fine. The "lulus" — payments in lieu of expenses — were nice to have; and the influence of the position was gratifying. But there was a point beyond which no Al Smith could rise. In the state and in the nation, the Democratic Party had been so frequently in the minority since the Civil War that it was hopeless for an Irish Catholic Tammany man to aspire to the topmost positions. Even when the party had held the Presidency or the governorship — as under Cleveland or Dix — the East Siders had been shunted to the rear. No one of their number had been governor or senator or even mayor of the consolidated city.

There was a kind of honor attached to these places for which men like themselves seemed unworthy. A governor or senator was expected to present an image — in appearance, speech and manners — appropriate to his high office. Somehow it was incongruous to think of an Irishman up from the city streets in such a post. Many well-meaning citizens, who would have denied indignantly that they were prejudiced, felt uncomfortable at the very thought. Indeed, often the Tammany men themselves, conservative when it came to matters of status, acquiesced in the judgment. Besides, in the practical matter of ticket-making, there was an advantage to putting a Protestant at the head; that way, the machine might pick up some outside votes while it could, in any case, count on the support of its own followers. Then too, in the judgment of the old-timers, there was no point to it. Big Tim Sullivan, for instance, had been bored as a congressman; Washington was too far away from the Bowery, he complained.

Some of the younger ones, of course, were beginning to wonder: Why not? They were native-born and had been to school and believed the talk about equality of opportunity. In America, they thought, every man had a chance, even to be President. One had only to look at the Legislature to see how it worked, how an Irish Catholic, Al Smith, and a German Protestant, Bob Wagner, and a Jew, Aaron Levy, got on together. Or take the constitutional convention where Al had been the respected colleague of Root and Wickersham and Wadsworth.

Maybe it was true. The men in the clubs wished to believe it. They talked back to the time when William R. Grace — a wealthy merchant and not really one of them, but an Irishman none the less — had been mayor of old New York. Well, then, some of them, like Smith, wished desperately to think it could happen now. But could they take the risk of acting as if it were really possible?

They looked earnestly for the signs of an affirmative answer. The fight over the United States senatorship in 1911 was a victory from that point of view. Though a Sheehan had lost, an O'Gorman had made it.

Murphy and the older men were cautious. There had been too many disappointments in their past and they were constitutionally averse to putting too much stock in ideals. Still, if there was a man among them who might someday go up, it was worth while grooming him for the eventuality. Al was the man.

Smith was in a strategic position, not only by virtue of his long and loyal service in the Legislature, but by virtue also of the new stature he had acquired in the constitutional convention. That he had earned the admiration of the respectable and conservative Republican lawyers and also of the many progressives carried a good deal of weight in the Hall. Here was a man who could be elected and — what was even more important — who could serve success-fully and with credit to his party and his group. Besides, he was already the most popular of Tammany speakers.

Some time in 1915 Murphy, with Foley's approval, decided to ready Smith for an important office. In his own district Al was unassailable; on "old home night," Oliver Street showered approval on its favorite son — and not only the Irish, but also the Greeks, Italians, Armenians, and Chinese, all in their native costumes. On the other hand, he had never campaigned from or been elected in any but his own ward. The first step was to put him up in a county-wide election.

In the spring and summer of that year, he began to speak from a variety of new platforms. He addressed the Real Estate Owners' Association and the Taxpayers' Alliance. He was making himself widely known, for he was a candidate for the office of sheriff of New York County. These aspirations were at first covert; it was never wise to seek a nomination too openly. Foley explained to the press that Smith's best interests lay elsewhere; and Murphy seemed to support "Big Bill" Edwards. The initiative in Al's designation came from the district leaders; but everyone, including Edwards, yielded with enthusiasm. Squeaking by the primary, he was elected in the fall with a handsome majority. The change in his reputation by then was so marked that he had the endorsement of the Citizens Union, the *Tribune,* the *Times,* the A.F. of L. and numerous social workers. This was a rare distinction for a Tammany candidate, and a demonstration that the good government forces would support a worthy candidate, whatever his party or origins.

As sheriff in 1916 and 1917, Al found the duties of office far from onerous. He later observed that he had spent most of his time "looking for something to do." For an ambitious young man, however, the position was highly strategic. The sheriff was still paid by an anachronistic fee system that brought him about fifty thousand dollars a year. Foley, who had himself held the office, warned him that the demands on the salary would be enormous "unless you want to give them all the marble heart." But still a tidy sum would be left to apply to expensive campaigning later. The patronage at his disposal was also useful in developing the basis of a personal organization. Smith participated in civil defense activities as the threat of war mounted. And as sheriff he got around, made speeches, testified at hearings, attended dinners, became known to the members of societies and the readers of newspapers. Al's wit, his capacity to attune himself to the taste of any audience, and his ability to be both convincing and interesting quickly spread his reputation through the city. He still found time, however, in November 1916, for old time's sake to take part in Boucicault's *The Shaughraun* in a benefit for the St. James parochial school.

By the middle of 1916, there was talk that Smith would soon move up to a more desirable place. He was then "the most popular man in the organization." One rumor had it that he would succeed Murphy as the head of Tammany, but the boss had no intention of retiring. It was more likely that Smith would run for a city-wide office in the campaign of 1917 and his name was often mentioned as a possible mayoralty candidate. Most of the district leaders seemed for him.

The larger political strategy that year called for another choice. Murphy intended to take no risks in getting rid of the hostile Mitchel administration. He wanted the wholehearted support of McCooey and the Brooklyn machine, of William Randolph Hearst, and of the German-American Democrats. John F. Hylan was therefore the nominee. Smith made no active effort to secure the place, but he did not eliminate himself as a possibility (there was no telling how the cards might fall), and his friends continued to speak for him until the selection was made. Then he was rewarded with the candidacy for the presidency of the Board of Aldermen. The whole ticket was elected without difficulty.

Smith served in this office for only one year of his four-year term. He then gained some useful insight into the city's problems, largely those of transit and public works. He spoke of the need for a better distribution system to lower the cost of living; and he argued "that the city should have the power to purchase, construct, own, and operate any public utility." But the board was not a body within which much could be done; most of its work was petty administrative detail. Al made some effort to increase its effectiveness within the limits set by state law; but his attention by the middle of 1918 was focused elsewhere. It seemed likely he would be the Democratic candidate for governor that fall.

The three years in municipal politics had pulled Al out of the narrow round of ward life in which, as assemblyman, he had still rotated. The campaigns of 1915 and 1917 had compelled him to make his name known to the whole city. He had developed the habit of public appearance. The outbreak of war found him explaining foreign policy, selling liberty loans, recruiting soldiers and home defense deputies, and otherwise maintaining his position in the public eye.

Yet, in these campaigns, Al had found it necessary to make no radical changes in his style. He became familiar with different men and new issues, but still retained the confidence that he could be elected for what he was and on his own basis.

Murphy was largely responsible for Smith's gubernatorial nomination, although he was too clever to show his hand openly. The initiative seemed to come from a meeting of upstate leaders, led by William F. Kelly of Syracuse. After preliminary maneuvers eliminated Hearst, who had the backing of McCooey's Brooklyn machine, and neutralized W. C. Osborn, the darling of the intransigent reformers, Smith was designated the organization candidate and won readily in the primaries. Support by Secretary of State Lansing and Secretary of the Treasury McAdoo was a sign of the approval of the national administration.

In 1918 Smith made the first of five campaigns for the governorship. He then defeated the incumbent Governor Whitman by a majority of fifteen thousand. In 1920, the Republican tide was too powerful. The suspicion of many Irish-Americans that the League of Nations was a British device to thwart Ireland's struggle for independence cost the Democrats crucial votes. Assurances by such organizations as the Irish-American Jeffersonian Union that the local ticket had no connection with the League issue went for nought; Smith lost to Nathan Miller. But he was back in 1922, with an overpowering victory.

Perhaps his greatest triumph came in 1924 when, despite the national strength of the G.O.P., he defeated Colonel Theodore Roosevelt, son of T.R., by a handsome margin. Al's achievement was particularly noteworthy by contrast with the outcome in Massachusetts, where James Michael Curley, a very different kind of politician, was swamped in the Coolidge tidal wave. In 1926 he was again successful, beating Ogden Mills without difficulty. By then he seemed well-nigh invincible in the state. "The man you run against ain't a candidate," wrote Will Rogers in an open letter, "he is just a victim."

In these campaigns Smith created a style and a method that made him New York's outstanding political figure and that ultimately earned him national stature. He drew together a group of devoted followers; he addressed himself to meaningful issues; and he developed a relationship to the electorate that gave him a high degree of security in office.

Already in 1918 the outlines of his organization were clear; and they became better defined with the passage of each election. The Tammany connection assured him a sweep of the city. Smith was able to maintain considerable independence of the machine and yet to count on its support, precisely because he was an insider, one of the boys who knew how the wheels turned.

He got along well enough with Murphy. The old leader died in April, 1924. Al was then able to dictate the choice of an acceptable successor, George W. Olvany. He could then also get rid of Hylan, Hearst's mayor. Unable to persuade either his friend James A. Foley or Robert Wagner to take on the job, Smith finally accepted James J. Walker as a candidate. A flitting leprechaun of a man, Walker had genuine ability — except when it came to staying out of trouble. He and the Governor maintained an uneasy relationship of mutual mistrust.

Al refused the support of William Randolph Hearst, whom he deprived, almost singlehandedly, of the senatorial nomination in 1922. The Governor also had a permanent falling-out with John Curry and Jimmy Hines, two powerful district leaders. But Smith did not pay the penalty of independence, because he had enough strength in the friendship of other sachems and because, in the last analysis, the machine could not turn against one of its own.

Smith had no desire to be simply a Tammany governor. He had shown that in his first campaign when he located upstate headquarters in Syracuse. He proceeded, therefore, quickly to develop dependable working arrangements with the Democratic organizations outside Manhattan. Ed Flynn of the Bronx went along, particularly after the election of Walker, who had been his candidate. There was some coolness, but outward friendliness, in the relationships with McCooey of Brooklyn, long a Hearst collaborator. In Albany, the O'Connell clan was just taking over and could use Al's help, even if they had to clean up the town — somewhat — in order to get it. The other upstate cities were still controlled by Republicans, although the Democratic organizations there, with the Governor's aid, were growing in strength. All these politicians needed him as much as he needed them and they knew it. That left him almost invulnerable.

Outside the formal party structure, Al created an organization of highly effective men and women, different from the run-of-the-mill campaigners. Few of them were stump orators able to descend to the bustle of electioneering. They performed other, more valuable, services. Most of them held places in his administration. From their knowledge of the state and from their experience in government he drew advice and material for his speeches. They thus helped him create a novel and efficient channel of communication by which he explained the affairs of the state to its citizens.

These people constituted an over-all board of strategy. Not that they ever met in any formality as a group. But they were available, as individuals or in twos and threes, when the Governor needed them, to serve on commissions, to draft bills, to listen to speeches, to dig up information, to consult on questions of strategy and policy.

On one level were certain old associates, who formed a corps of elder statesmen, as it were. Murphy and Tom

Foley were consulted on political matters until their deaths in 1924 and 1925. Bob Wagner had become a justice of the state Supreme Court in 1919, but remained on intimate terms with Smith until he left for Washington and the Senate in 1927.

Three other judges put their wisdom and experience at the Governor's service. James A. Foley was a New Yorker, but of a somewhat different background from Al. Ten years younger, he had had the opportunity to go to City College and to New York Law School. The two men had come to value one another in the Legislature, where Foley served between 1907 and 1919, when he was elected surrogate. Preferring the calm of the bench to the turmoil of active politics, he turned down opportunities to be leader of Tammany, mayor, and United States senator. Judicious by temperament and deeply learned in the law, he had the respect of the whole circle for his knowledge of the state and its problems.

Abram I. Elkus was already a distinguished attorney when he had become counsel for the Factory Commission. Tom Foley had been among his clients; and he had early come to know and value the future Governor. Elkus had later been congressman, and Ambassador to Turkey. In 1918 he formed an Independent Citizens' Committee in support of Smith's candidacy and helped manage the campaign. He moved on to the Court of Appeals, but retained his active interest in Smith's work.

His law partner, Joseph M. Proskauer, also in time became a judge. Born in Mobile, Proskauer had been a student at Columbia College. From James Harvey Robinson and George Edward Woodberry he had acquired an interest in history and literature, a concern with spiritual

values, and a humane attitude toward contemporary problems. Proskauer had stayed on in New York to develop a
lucrative practice. But he was always involved in philanthropy, and his activity in the Citizens' Union drew him
into politics. He quickly became one of Al's most intimate
advisers.

More active, because they were in more continuous contact with the Governor, were the members of a somewhat
younger group. George R. Van Namee of Watertown,
another lawyer, was a friend from back in Smith's days in
the Legislature. He became the Governor's secretary in
1919 and a year later found an important berth on the
Public Service Commission. His unrivaled knowledge of
state departments and of personnel everywhere stood Al
in good stead.

His successor as the Governor's assistant was Belle Moskowitz. Belle had been Mrs. Israels when Al first heard of
her, the widow of a prominent architect, interested in social
welfare and once a member of the staff of the Educational
Alliance. She had long been concerned with the labor
problem and for a time had been active in the short-lived
Progressive Party. In 1914 she had married Henry Moskowitz, whom Smith had met after the Triangle fire and
who had since remained involved in liberal politics. Elkus
and Proskauer, who had known her at the Alliance, found
a place for her on Smith's staff in 1918. Alert, critical and
well-informed, she came to be his most valued assistant.

Mrs. Moskowitz brought into the group a young Yale
graduate and a Republican who had worked a while for
the Bureau of Municipal Research. While Smith had
been out of office, in 1921 and 1922, he came to know
Robert Moses well. The two would walk down to Oliver

Street together and spend hours talking about government. When Al returned to office, Moses entered the state's service and ultimately became Secretary of State. By nature Moses was an engineer, with all the engineer's display of realism and scientific precision. That made him an effective administrator. But like many engineers he was at heart a dreamer whose facts and figures clothed daring projects. Abrupt, frank — sometimes to the point of rudeness — and thoroughly honest, he was a superb lieutenant to the Governor.

Smith created an atmosphere that enabled these people to work together. This was not simply a matter of his loyalty to the staff, of his absolute dependability and the radiant good humor that kept the office sparkling and humming. More important was his ability to communicate to those around him a sense of the importance of their efforts. Somebody would come up with a frustrating legalism, some obscure case of *Grabenheimer* v. *the People;* or with a Websterism that made a word more important than a principle. Well, that was not something one stood around about or accepted idly. One worked it out, for the enterprise in which all were engaged had significance and dignity and demanded a man's best.

In the continuing interchange with these people, Smith sharpened his own ideas. He did not simply borrow from them; the process was reciprocal, with his practical knowledge rubbing against their formal education and book-learning. Often he and they would start with markedly divergent views and argue bitterly, with voices growing louder and fists pounded on the table, until the rightness of the matter became clear. And there was no pain in giving in, or self-congratulation in winning out; there was

shared satisfaction enough for all in the goals being attained.

This process defined a political position to which Smith
adhered with some constancy in the ten years after 1918.
He was no philosopher and never evolved a theoretical
system; but a thread of coherent beliefs held together his
statements as concrete issues arose in campaign after
campaign.

Most Americans imagined that the outstanding political
issue of the decade was Prohibition; and every politician
longed to straddle the issue. Smith had no wish to antagonize either the fanatical "Drys" or the fiery "Wets."
But he was particularly vulnerable. His opponents were
quick to label a Tammany man the tool of the gambling
and liquor interests and that compelled him to take a
stand on the question. In any case, pressure from his
organization and his own convictions made him forthright.

What, Al wondered, had induced the government thus
to meddle with the personal habits of its citizens? He did
not take seriously the denunciations of the corner saloon
by those who had never entered one; he himself had spent
many a pleasant hour in those "dens of iniquity" and without pretense he continued to have a cheering glass when
he felt like it. Rather, Prohibition was the product of
the reformers' tendency wishfully to pretend that a new
law could change the character of the world, and to use
that pretense to impose their own tastes upon others.

The hypocrisy of it offended Smith. He saw the evidence
in such politicians as Governor Whitman who had campaigned Dry, while personally bibulous. More important,

the prohibitionists had deliberately omitted any definition of "intoxicating beverage" from the Eighteenth Amendment in order to assure its passage, and then proceeded to establish a restrictive and narrow definition by Act of Congress. Within the state, the people had never had the opportunity to express themselves on the question. Smith called first for a more realistic conception of what "intoxicating" meant and then for repeal.

Much of the animus generated by the issue, Smith understood, was really directed against people like himself. The saloon was evil because it was situated in the city and was frequented by the Irish. Prohibition thus gave expression to the anti-Catholicism widespread in the rural sections of the state. Smith encountered the religious issue in the campaign of 1918; and it plagued him in every election thereafter.

He fought prejudice squarely; compromise was inconceivable. He could not counter ugly charges secretly made. But he could eloquently affirm his faith in Americanism. This, for him, was more than a matter of fife-and-drum patriotism; it was also a way of life that encouraged the diversity he had known from the time he was a boy on the East Side and that evaluated a man for what he was — otherwise, he would himself never have climbed out of the day laborer's drudgery. Hence he would make no pretense about himself, about his sidewalk origins, about his Irish loyalties.

He defended the immigrants feelingly, because he knew them from having lived among them, but also because they were the symbols of his America, which God had hidden behind a veil from the corruption of Europe until it was time for the prow of the *Santa Maria* "to open to the world a haven for the oppressed." It was of the essence of this nation that men should be regarded for what they were rather than for what their antecedents had been. For they were all evolving toward a common destiny of liberty. Al could himself remember how the cops at the Oak Street Station had boycotted the first Negro patrolman, then had come to accept and like him so that he could in time rise to the rank of captain.

Americans were also able to rise above other social distinctions that divided rich from poor or skilled from unskilled labor and obscured the common interests of all. Let the socialists, misled by their delusions, talk their heads off about the "class struggle." The facts of life were against them. "The bricklayer couldn't draw $6 a day if he had to carry the bricks," Al pointed out. In the same way, "irresponsible and wanton attacks on business" were "a blow to capital and labor alike. The prosperity of the working-man" depended "in large part upon the prosperity of the employer."

What was important was not the class or group but the individual. That was the theme of many a popular song and story, of the great romances of the stage and the flickering screen. If you had a man you loved him so, whatever he may be; and Abie got his Rose with no Irish hostility. Why, this was America where everyone had a chance to be a Yankee Doodle Dandy.

Yes, it was the individual for whom society and government existed. That was why smaller units of control were preferable to larger ones. Home rule for cities and states' rights gave the people a better opportunity to judge what was good for them. But the main thing was how power was used, not how it was distributed. If the state was wasteful and unnecessarily burdened its citizens with high taxes and restrictive laws, it failed in its function. On the other hand, it failed equally if it did not function at all. Here was a mechanism that could be made to work efficiently as a means toward the end of improving all the individuals in the society. The government could build a barge canal and highways to help the whole economy. For the same reason it could help agriculture "produce more crops and less politics." It could also develop power resources and other public utilities, not out of commitment to any ideology, but when such projects seemed advantageous to all.

It did not contract, but rather expanded men's liberties, if the state protected those who were incapable of protecting themselves. By sustaining public education, it expanded human resources. In periods of high and rising prices, the government had an obligation to intervene to lower the cost of living. In good times as well as bad, it ought to aid the dependent, not able to fend for themselves. The conditions of labor for women and children, the welfare of the widowed and the aged, were of right the constant concern of the state.

These ideas carried a refreshing breath of hope through the battered ranks of the progressives. All the surviving crusaders for old causes were now in his camp: Thomas Mott Osborne and Franklin Delano Roosevelt of the Sheehan fight; Chester C. Platt, a Sulzerite; old Bull Moose; battlers for the New Freedom; former socialists; insurgent Republicans; and Independents of many a hue. The women, who now wielded the ballot in their own right, were particularly drawn to Al, although he had long opposed the extension of the suffrage to their sex. It was not only the prominence of Frances Perkins and Belle Moskowitz in his administration that attracted them, nor even the special campaigns directed at their votes; but rather the overwhelming persuasiveness of his humanitarianism and of his faith in the power of education.

Since the beginning of the century the progressives had enlisted in one crusade after another. Yet all their effort, enthusiasm, and thought had brought them into the dull decade of the 1920's. What had the great victories that had enacted so many reforms produced but the administrations of Harding and Coolidge, with their dismaying corruption and their constant pandering to the materialism of a people blinded by the appearance of prosperity! A valiant handful of insurgents in the Senate continued to fight a rearguard action; but few among them had the vision of a positive program that could generate widespread enthusiasm.

To the gloomy and disheartened, Smith's voice, charged with faith and sincerity, brought a prospect of recovery. True he had been a Tammany man. But in a way that added to the impressiveness of his achievement; for so many years he had carried pitch and remained unsmeared. He had grown as Tammany had not; and, undeniably, he knew the business of government. Furthermore, he had not been committed to the old progressivism and therefore did not bear the burden of its defeats or — what was even worse — of victories that led only to disappointment. Men of many shades of political opinion saw in him the embodiment of a new liberalism, practical, rooted in the cities, and willing to confront the problems of an industrial society. He was far from being what all these anxious people thought he was. But there was enough in the program for which he spoke to lend substance to their dreams.

Al's voice carried to another audience, a larger and more significant one. In the 1920's, the children and the grand-children of the immigrants were reaching political ma-turity. As they acquired education and skill, moved up-ward on the educational ladder and outward away from the slums, they became concerned about their place in American society. For more than two decades, they had been under attack in the long debate over immigration restriction — stigmatized as members of inferior races, barred from desirable trades, and challenged as to their capacity for citizenship. Now their numbers had grown and with it a potential of political power, still unrecognized by the old-line politicians. Smith was one of them, up from the city streets, and his career was the living demon-stration of the falsity of the accusations against them. They were certainly predisposed to listen, because he was "the incarnation of their own hope and pride."

And what he said made sense to men and women who had their own recollections of the slums, whose childhood friends, or perhaps parents, still carried the hod or toiled at the sewing machine. They knew what widowhood or illness meant to those who lived without margin; and the high cost of living to them was no empty abstraction.

Through the decade Smith profited by the stupidity of old-guard Republican leadership that refused to see that the Jews, the Italians, the Poles, and the French Canadians were becoming a political factor of consequence. Louis Marshall, who knew the immigrants, warned his party, the G.O.P., that these people "resent the idea that they are to be treated as inferiors," and asked for the acts of "human kindness" that Tammany understood and that were responsible for Smith's great political success. But the Republican Party was intractable and went no further than empty gestures that only confirmed the growing loyalty of the newer groups to one they felt spoke for them.

This audience Smith knew how to address. Anyone could tell the Italians or the Irish about their glorious contribution to American civilization. But Al knew that what they really wanted from the spoken word was conviction. Therefore, he insisted that his pledges and his speeches tell the truth and be rigidly adhered to. His platform appearance conveyed sincerity and authenticity. His voice was somewhat raucous and thick with the accent of the East Side; and he disdained the orator's tricks of modulation. He was an actor without mask or pretense. He knew what he was and he had something to say that people wanted to hear, and they listened.

Knowing that they listened he could make them hear. "My friends," he would say, "let us look at the record"; and he knew the record. He had no hesitation in calling on the services of academic experts; his staff made data available to him; and he acquired the habit of accumulating the material for future speeches in envelopes. Although he spoke readily and easily and had a prodigious memory for facts and figures, he was careful in preparation. He knew that the first test of the actor was to know his lines. Although he did not read from or confine himself to a text, he usually dictated his speeches in advance so that he could "walk through the part," try them out on his Board of Strategy or on Herbert Bayard Swope, editor of the *World*. When, as in 1926, his opponents were not as well prepared as he, he made a spectacle of their ignorance of state government.

Above all, Smith had the ability to make complex issues dramatic and understandable. Sensitive to the mood of his audience, he knew how to get across. His sentences were short and direct, loaded with figures of speech from everyday life, that brought the problems of state home to the men and women before him. From Tom Grady he had once heard of Horatio Seymour's knack with statistics: "Why, he could make tangled figures concerning cubic yards in the Erie Canal sound like a romance. He presented them in such shape that you'd think Dickens was reading one of his novels." Al took this comment to heart and in time outdid the great Democratic orators of the past. He "could make statistics sit up, beg, roll over and bark," said one of his staff.

The people listened and understood. At the end of each session he gave a popular accounting of state expenditures; and he made it thoroughly comprehensible — even exciting. While he was out of office in 1921, he was invited back to Albany to speak to the Legislature on the problems of the Port of New York; the charwomen crowded into the chamber to hear his two-hour analysis. And what he said got across. In 1927, the voters of the state were presented with nine amendments on a long ballot. Smith favored all but Number 6; and in the campaign explained why. Number 6 alone was defeated.

Smith's connection with the people was more than verbal; he never permitted himself to be isolated in the capital. In 1918, he had established campaign headquarters in the Hotel Biltmore, opposite Grand Central Station. He maintained a suite there for the next decade.

All sorts of people congregated there. You might say it was a kind of club, halfway between the Bowery and

Albany. A lot of fellows from downtown would come up just to hang around, perhaps in the hope of catching a word with one of the district leaders, who in turn were there to maybe take up a little matter with the Governor. These visitors often ran into one of Smith's staff leading in tow a social worker, or lawyer or professor, ready to be an expert on this problem or that. Aspiring politicians and citizens with political interests looked in now and then; it didn't hurt to be seen.

But of course it wasn't that organized. Usually there was a dog around, for the Governor retained his boyish love of pets (and had a zoo full of beasts up in Albany). Katie was as likely to be there as not; and a lot of her women friends dropped in, and sometimes their husbands were with them. Nobody remained a stranger very long in the cheerful turmoil.

Al would come in, pretty much as he had always been, somewhat grayer, a little more dignified, but the same good fellow as ever. He remained a snappy dresser; he always felt "spiffy" when he was "dressed just right." But he resisted changes in style and clung to the brown derby that was the sign of elegance in his youth. He was exuberant in the manner of a man who always had time for a good word and a slap on the back. It took little, when he was feeling good, to set him off in a song and dance or to get him to recite "Cohen on the Telephone" or "The Face on the Barroom Floor."

Yet beyond the bounce and jollity he had also the air of one who got things done. He did not lose touch with life, for his own experience had been all of a piece from the East Side to the Governor's Mansion. There had been no break in continuity, only a wider and wider audience at each stage of his career.

Of course, he had changed. While he was president of the Board of Aldermen he was still to be seen hanging around Foley's saloon; he could not continue to do so as Governor, and anyway, Prohibition had closed the saloon. In 1923, when Smith returned to the Executive Mansion, he gave up the place on Oliver Street. If thereafter the occasions for going downtown grew less frequent, still, to rise in the world was just progress.

In 1921 and 1922, in the interval out of office, he took a job as Chairman of the Board of the United States Trucking Company. Well, then he was something of a businessman and he acquired business friends, many of them Irish-Americans like himself. James J. Riordan, president of the company, for instance, had been born in Greenwich Village and had come up from being a truckdriver and bank teller. Out of love for Al, he would one day buy the house on Oliver Street as a memorial. "Uncle George" F. Getz of Chicago also held a share of U.S. Trucking, along with holdings in coal, banking, and hotels. He had met Smith in French Lick and, swayed by their common enthusiasm for zoos, offered him the position at fifty thousand dollars a year. James J. Hoey, who had been born on the East Side, but grew up in the Black Hills where his father worked on the railroad, now was a prosperous insurance man interested in politics and boys' clubs. Tim Mara had made his start as an errand boy and had had a hard time as a bookmaker before he became a big-time stockbroker.

At the center of this group was William F. Kenny, who had known Al slightly as a boy but now became his most intimate personal friend. His start had been driving an ash cart and he had put in time working in the slaughter-houses. Now he was an enormously wealthy contractor who had built practically everything the New York Edison owned and who had gotten in on the ground floor in automobiles and radio. The proud proprietor of the *St. Nicholas*, most expensive private car on the American railroads, it was his pleasure to take the Governor riding.

These wealthy, successful men of a background similar to his own gave Al a circle of cronies. They played golf together, or met for celebrations in the Tiger Room on the top floor of Kenny's building at the corner of Twenty-third Street and Fourth Avenue.

Through them, Al met all sorts of other people. Mara was owner of the New York Football Giants; and he and Getz were interested in promoting Gene Tunney's fights. That was a connection with the heroes of the world of sport, mostly poor kids too, like Babe Ruth and Gertrude Ederle, coming up from the city streets. At the Banshee Club, now and then, Smith had lunch with Gene Buck, songwriter for Florenz Ziegfeld; and he knew Al Jolson and many another star who made popular the songs all America sang.

It made him proud sometimes to see the influence of New York stretch out across the nation. Everybody was doing it, doing it. The Yale boys coming in for the week end, the old crowd in all the thousands of country clubs, the young crowd in the fraternity houses, the readers of newspapers, the watchers at movies, the listeners to the radio — all were vibrating to the New York beat. You couldn't keep them down on the farm. Why, Al had once said, I'd rather be a lamppost on Park Row than Governor of California. Here was the center of things, and everywhere else they were just waiting to be shaken up.

There were uncomfortable moments, no doubt, as when his sons Alfred Jr. and Arthur married too hastily and not as well as their father would have liked. On the other hand, the favorite daughter, Emily, married Major John A. Warner, a Republican and a graduate of Harvard, but a fine man at that. Catherine, in 1928, became the wife of Francis J. Quillinan, and Walter, the baby, was coming along fine.

Al's mother died in 1924. But the thought of her — as custodian of faith and rightness — stayed with him always. Like the mother in a favorite play: "Why, when she's worried she just reads the Bible a while — and then all her troubles go and she's happy again, because she says it makes her believe everything is going to be all right and then it is."

Everything was all right. The decade between 1918 and 1928 was made happy by the satisfaction with a job well done. Smith's record as Governor justified the passing years. He had earned a place in the galaxy of those who had made good, who had come up, who had made real the American dream of individual achievement.

V

Chief Executive

IT WAS A PROUD THING to be governor, almost the culmination of a career, and particularly so for a man of Smith's origins. The triumph had been not merely personal: it had also recognized the arrival of the sons of the immigrants and the maturity of the political forces they represented. Al was fully conscious of his position and was determined to administer the office in a manner that would be thoroughly creditable — to himself and to the group from which he had sprung. He went to Albany with the fixed determination "that never again would anybody be able to raise their head up in this state and say that the man from lower New York that belonged to Tammany Hall could not run the State." For ten years he held steadfastly to that purpose.

Smith was an effective chief executive. Official ceremonial duties weighed lightly upon him and he maintained his political contacts without strain or excessive sacrifice of time. Conscientious in his attention to the business of his office, he won general admiration for the way in which he conducted its affairs.

The prevailing prosperity of these years was a great help, of course. Despite a slight recession after the war and despite persistent pockets of discontent in the agricultural regions, the state's industry thrived, its wealth increased, and that eased many problems of government.

Still, it was no easy matter to conduct the affairs of the nation's largest state which grew in population from ten to twelve million during the decade. Its people held markedly diverse interests. About half of them were concentrated in the great metropolis on the Hudson; they lived by trade, finance and light manufacturing. Industry occupied the chain of upstate cities — Albany, Schenectady, Syracuse, Rochester, and Buffalo; and the urban problems of all these places frequently became part of the business of the state. Constitutional provisions and firmly held traditions strictly circumscribed the powers of the municipalities and frequently compelled the legislature and the governor to turn their attention to the needs of the residents of these places. The state often had to deal with such local questions as health, transit, power and utilities; and those became more difficult as the cities continued to grow.

At the same time, a large part of New York was still rural; and although the countryside held but a minority of the population an unequal allocation of legislative seats made it politically powerful out of all proportion to its numbers. No administration could afford to neglect the affairs of the agricultural element. The state government in the past had failed utterly in the attempt to cope with the complexity of these problems. Since the beginning of the century there had been only one successful administration, that of Charles Evans Hughes, and that only in a negative sense It had halted some of the more obvious abuses, but it was brief in duration; and it left behind few permanent accomplishments. Under one party or the other, New York had long been a mess, a striking contrast to state government elsewhere.

Smith's four terms of office changed the whole situation; he left to his successors a political structure capable of acting effectively in the interests of the people.

In making appointments and dealing with the general problems of patronage, Al had the enormous advantage of relative freedom from machine dictation. After his election Tom Foley had told him to do his best. "I have given everybody orders to lay off and give you a chance to do your duty." Precisely because Tammany knew that he would give its interests due consideration, he evaded the difficulties that had proved disastrous for Dix, Sulzer and Glynn. His solid control over appointments put him in a position of undisputed authority in the Democratic Party and, at the same time, enabled him to choose a competent administrative staff, disregarding party lines when necessary. Not a few of his appointments were genuinely nonpartisan, as when he made Robert Moses Secretary of State, Frances Perkins Industrial Commissioner, and Colonel Frederick S. Greene superintendent of the highway department.

Having an efficient staff, Smith was willing to rely upon it. He worried over such matters as pardons; but the ability to delegate power freed him from most bothersome routine details. His own loyalty to those who served him drew from them a devotion that amounted to dedication. They worked for a man who could be counted on to be absolutely candid, who never went back on his word, and who gave unqualified support to projects of which he approved. That was worth a good deal. There was even a kind of reassurance in knowing that if the Governor caught an error or disapproved of a line of action, or if political considerations made a change necessary, he would say so openly to one's face and keep nothing up his sleeve.

Experience had taught Smith that his predecessors had gone astray when they confined their attention to the Executive Mansion and disregarded what went on in the Senate and Assembly. The Governor had to be involved in the process of enacting the laws. Administration and legislation were inextricably intertwined. There was, of course, annually the matter of appropriations; and every departmental program depended for effective execution upon new laws to carry it through. Besides, some administrative boards and agencies were actually responsible to the legislature rather than to the governor. It was of the utmost importance to devise means of co-operation.

Alas for the prospect for collaboration; both the Assembly and the Senate were Republican in these years. The failure of redistricting to give New York City its due weight in state affairs made that inevitable. And the G.O.P. was not anxious to lighten Al's load. The Legislature, the Citizens' Union reported after his first term, showed "an unremitting opposition to anything Governor Smith wanted or suggested, and a determination to pass any measure, no matter how bad, if it might have the result of 'putting him in a hole' by forcing him to take a stand for or against it."

That obstructionist attitude, entirely understandable in terms of political strategy, persisted through Smith's tenure of office. Fortunately he had the means of circumventing it. He had long since learned how to deal with the opposition party. On the one hand he made maximum demands for the sake of the record. On the other, he was ever ready to compromise. No one he knew ever got anywhere by thinking that "he and his set and his party" had "all the virtue and all the goodness" in the world and that "everybody who doesn't agree with him is conniving to tear down the capitol."

It worked. Smith made it a practice to hold regular conferences with the legislative leaders, many of whom had been his friends from the old days. Sometimes it was possible to talk a measure back and forth and reach an agreement, or at least an understanding of differences in viewpoint. And when it came to a showdown, Smith had the courage to use three potent weapons. On three occasions he forced the recalcitrant legislators into the extra sessions they disliked. He vetoed bills of which he disapproved; and not one of his vetoes was ever overridden. And he could use the weight of public opinion to compel the intransigent Republicans to follow along in his wake. Fear of his consistent popularity throughout the state and of his ability to present his case to the people won him many a vote in the Assembly and Senate. In 1925, annoyed by a deadlock, he called forty newspapermen to dinner and laid his case on the line. "Napoleon's retreat from Moscow was as nothing compared with the return from Albany of the defeated, discomfited, disgraced Republican hosts" that followed. Soon the G.O.P. legislators learned he was not to be trifled with; time and again they "complained but complied" because they knew he held the trump cards.

In every aspect of political life legislation and action were interrelated. Even the narrow conduct of the governor's office could be effective only if new statutes reshaped the administrative branches of the state government. As New York had grown, the state had taken on a multitude of new functions, each of which called for additional machinery. The number of agencies had consequently risen with dismaying rapidity. It was easy to create new boards; and it was hard to abolish old ones, even when their functions had all but disappeared. Furthermore, these offshoots had sprouted without plan or order. The Legislature, in bringing them into being, had rarely thought of their place in the context of the total structure of the state government. Each bureau had its own mode of organization and procedure. Many department heads were not responsible to the governor; and in the general confusion it was difficult to know how the lines of authority ran. When Smith first took office, one hundred and sixty-nine different agencies, appointed by sixteen different procedures, and removable in seven different ways, shared the chaotic, overlapping administration of the state. Even conscientious governors like Hughes had stumbled in the past in the effort to bring some order into this situation.

Smith was prepared to deal with the problem. As an assemblyman, he had already become aware of the tangled network of governmental relationships; and in the Constitutional Convention he had pleaded for the total recasting of the machinery of administration. Now his opportunity came. He sought consistently to apply two principles to the problem: first, the orderly arrangement of all agencies in departments, the heads of which reported to the governor; and then, the definite location of authority and responsibility in individuals who would be free to do their jobs but who would be held accountable for them.

In his very first message, he announced the creation of a

Reconstruction Commission to plan the effective coordination of state functions. The commission, of which Abram Elkus was chairman and Belle Moskowitz secretary, recruited an able staff of experts led by Robert Moses. Privately financed when the Legislature refused it funds, it produced a far-ranging program for political, economic, and social reform and planning. It also proposed a scheme for consolidating departments and bringing them under the supervision of the chief executive. Delaying tactics by the Republicans, however, postponed action for years. Smith continued to agitate for reform, meanwhile making what piecemeal changes he could.

In 1925, the Legislature could put off action no longer. By a majority of almost 60 per cent, the voters ratified a series of amendments approving reorganization. The size of the majority showed that the people were being educated to the importance of the subject. The Legislature had no intention of yielding gracefully, however. If change was indeed inevitable it was determined to have it on Republican rather than on Democratic terms. It therefore created a new Reorganization Commission, on which Smith's enemies were heavily represented.

The maneuver helped them not in the least. An open letter from the Governor suggested that Charles Evans Hughes be chairman of the commission; and even the most adamant Republican could not bypass the distinguished lawyer, former governor, secretary of state, justice of the Supreme Court, and Republican candidate for the Presidency. Hughes took the assignment seriously; and his report sustained the ideas for which Smith had long fought. A law effective in 1927 created sixteen comprehensive departments within which all administrative functions were reorganized. Another measure improved the structure of the judiciary.

Efforts to get the Legislature to reform its own procedure made little headway. The representatives remained engrossed in the "minor, little detail" measures that affected their own districts and paid little attention, except for the Governor's prodding, to the big questions. In 1926 fifty-two different amendments were made to the fish and game laws, Smith pointed out, while a thirty-two-million-dollar highway bill got only perfunctory attention. "Who in the whole state is sufficiently interested in the size of a walleyed pike to have to define its dimensions by law before you can take it?"

By contrast, there were significant steps toward recasting the archaic forms of local government inherited "from the days when the king had something to say around here." Smith retained the interest in municipal home rule that he and other Tammany men had developed when they had smarted under upstate control of the City of New York. In the interests of clear definition of functions, he refused to exercise powers he felt the governor ought not to have; and he gave his blanket approval to laws desired by local authorities. Largely at his insistence, a home-rule amendment in 1923 began the process of urban emancipation. To the same end, he encouraged the diversion to the cities and counties of larger shares of the income and other state-collected taxes. The amount so disbursed rose from six to sixty million dollars between 1918 and 1928.

These achievements won Smith widespread recognition among progressives interested in governmental efficiency. Low costs that kept waste and taxation to a minimum were the measure of the effective state; and Smith took pride in the restrained tax rate of his administrations. Indeed, he was willing to go much farther than the Legislature would allow him in reducing the burden upon low-income groups.

Inevitably also he faced the problem of reordering the state's finances. The Governor had no desire to save money at the expense of a single worthwhile activity. But he insisted that every dollar appropriated be "absolutely necessary for the proper conduct of the business of the state." Above all he wanted a dependable system of expenditures. He was troubled from the start by the caprice of the Legislature which turned alternatively to taxation and bond issues as the sway of political vagaries dictated. The Republicans were using "a little catch phrase, 'Pay as you go.'" That was fine. But the great trouble was "that we do not pay and we do not go." Al thought that permanent improvements ought never to come out of current revenues, while current costs ought never to be financed by long-term loans. If capital charges were separated out from the annual ones, the state could operate on an orderly and solvent basis which would still not hamper it in essential matters. It could also develop continuing programs for public works spread out over many years.

As a necessary first step Smith resumed the struggle for an executive budget that he had already begun in the Constitutional Convention. The arguments he had developed in 1915 had even greater relevance from the perspective of the governor's chair. At session after session he repeated the request, and finally wore down the Legislature in 1927. The executive budget, together with the improvement in state finances and the reorganization of administrative departments, gave New York an efficient structure of state government by the time Smith left office in 1928.

The purpose of an instrument was to be used; as the mechanism improved, Smith eagerly sought to put it to work to help the people of the state. It was not easy to do so when it came to agriculture. The Governor was certainly sensitive to the necessity of placating the farmers already pinched by depression and always suspicious of him as a city man. But he himself had had little experience with the problem, and a farm bloc in the Legislature obstructed his every move. An investigation in 1923 exposed the pattern of control by agricultural interests in a department headed "by a floorwalker from an Elmira dry goods store." Yet Smith was virtually helpless until the administrative reorganization four years later. "I am in the the anomalous position of being without power or responsibility," he repeatedly complained. It took a struggle to get the state to pay even for killing tubercular cows. The larger difficulties of the farmer were, in any case, national and international in scope. The state alone could do nothing about overproduction, low prices, and credit stringency.

Smith had already become familiar with the problems of natural resources in the Constitutional Convention, where he had worked with ardent conservationists like Louis Marshall. Al had no sentimental feelings about the preservation of wildlife. God made birds and beasts and fish to be eaten, or to be kept in the zoo or aquarium. But Smith understood the need to protect the state's interests against those who wished heedlessly to exploit its forests and streams.

It took an effort of the imagination to move from a static conception of conservation to a more dynamic view of the state's responsibility for recreation. Smith was in favor of parks, for instance; but a park was a lot of grass in the center of the city where the kids could play. The idea of setting apart large tracts of wild land as parks roused no enthusiasm in him. From that point of view, the whole state outside Manhattan was a park! There was no point to spending public funds on playgrounds that would serve only a few. "You want to give the people a fur overcoat," he said to Robert Moses, "when what they need is red flannel underwear." Necessities came before luxuries.

By 1923, however, Moses had convinced him that access to the open spaces of nature had value to the whole population. Thereafter he threw himself vigorously into the task of creating a network of parks and beaches from Long Island to Niagara Falls. In 1923 he persuaded the Legislature to agree to a policy of systematic annual appropriations for development. A year later, a fifteen-million-dollar bond issue supplied the funds for the beginnings of expansion.

Once involved, he was in the fight wholeheartedly. Some of the Long Islanders, reluctant to have a public park set down in the midst of their estates, got the Legislature to throw the book at him. There was no appropriation and without cash available there could be no condemnation proceedings. Well, that didn't stop the Governor; he wheedled two hundred and fifty thousand dollars out of August Hecksher and went ahead anyway.

The shift in attitude was not altogether surprising. The parks were coming closer to the cities as the number of automobiles mounted with staggering rapidity. But that, in turn, put an unexpected strain upon the highway system. The inability of local communities to manage either the costs or the planning of modern roads compelled the state to act. Smith believed that such projects should be financed by taxation. But he was not niggardly and was willing to put the government's support behind them. In 1920 a law permitted the state to aid in the construction of county highways, and that set in motion a long-term program of development.

The rising volume of traffic created a host of subsidiary problems. New roads conflicted with the right of way of railroads, as the dramatic wreck of the Twentieth Century Limited in the heart of Syracuse showed in 1923. Before grade crossings could be eliminated, it was necessary to decide who should do the work and who should bear the expense. A three-hundred-million-dollar bond issue, authorized in 1925, enabled the state to share the cost with the railroads and with local communities. Reforms in traffic law, regulation of motor vehicles, licensing of drivers, efforts to develop rural express service and to improve the Barge Canal, and the appointment of an Aviation Commission showed Smith's awareness of the significance of new developments in transportation.

Long-standing precedents left no question as to the competence of the government to build and maintain highways. But Smith's suggestion that municipalities be allowed to own and operate transit, power and other utilities were bitterly and successfully resisted by the private companies and by those who rejected in principle the extension of state authority into these spheres. Even the Citizens' Union condemned these proposals as "state socialism."

Yet it was not easy to draw the line between what was public and what was private, as the difficulty of exploiting the state's water power showed. The spread in the use of electricity had early led to demands that the Saint Lawrence and the streams of the Adirondacks be harnessed for power. At the beginning of the century the rights of development had casually been given to private enterprises. The disregard for the state's interests in these grants had however evoked protests, especially from the conservationists; and Democratic legislatures between 1911 and 1913 had put a halt to the practice.

For Smith the question involved more than preservation of the beauty of mountain streams. His larger concern was to secure the maximum development of electricity at rates advantageous to the people. As minority leader in the Assembly in 1914, he had pointed to the dangers of permitting private companies to lay their hands upon the state's most important resources. He saw three possible modes of using the power sites: grants to corporations; government development with operating leases to private concerns; and government ownership, development and operation. The third most adequately served the larger interests of the society; water power was "the property of all the people," who should themselves be the beneficiaries of its use. "There was the meat in the coconut."

Republican capture of the state in 1914, however, had put the shaping of policy in other hands. The Machold Storage Law, a year later, authorized river-regulating districts to lease power sites to private firms at terms most advantageous to the companies. Smith failed in the effort to reverse that decision in 1919 and in 1920. The Legislature further consolidated the principle of private exploitation when it set up a commission specifically authorized to lease away the state's resources.

The conflict came to a crisis in 1926. The commission, dominated by Republicans, had held hearings through that year on the petition of several companies for rights on the Saint Lawrence. When Smith learned that it was ready to make the award at a final session on December 8, he determined to block the give-away. He asked the commission to delay its action. The Governor knew he had popular approval; the November election, in which the power issue had been prominent, had shown that. Furthermore a reorganization of the state departments was due to bring into office a new agency whose members he would himself appoint.

For the very same reason, of course, the commission refused to put off the decision. At this point Smith acted vigorously. He appointed Samuel Untermyer as special counsel and announced that he would contest the validity of any grant through the courts. Faced with the prospect of endless litigation, the applicants withdrew.

By then, the proper solution was clear in Al's own mind. Each year, from 1924 through 1928, he asked the Legislature to create a State Power Authority — a public corporation like the Port Authority — able to develop the state's power resources. The Republicans obstinately refused. But ten years of battle had produced some results: the Governor had protected the best sites; he had enlightened the people about the nature of the problem; and he had prepared the ground for the positive achievements of his successors.

Above all, however, Smith was engaged by the problems of social legislation. Himself a product of the East Side, he understood the needs of the working population of the cities. His experience in the Assembly had already drawn him into battle against those "steeped in Bourbonism," who regarded only property rights with solicitude and who believed "that our great human resources must take care of themselves" with no protection from the state. As Governor he continued to maintain the obligation of the government to assist the most necessitous of its citizens.

The labor problem never frightened Al. He had faith in the worker's desire to earn his bread by an honest day's toil and faith also that the economy would reward those who deserved it. There was an outbreak of disturbing strikes in 1919 when he took office. But that was "an extraordinary situation" due to a "cyclical depression." He appointed mediators for some of the conflicts, set up a board to study the causes of unrest, and created state employment bureaus to relieve the difficulty until the return of better times. Unions would be law-abiding and responsible bodies once the legitimate grievances of their members were satisfied.

In the immediate aftermath of the war, high prices were the greatest threat to the wage earner; and the one cost, rent, which none could escape, was the greatest burden of all. Building costs had trebled between 1915 and 1920; and through the next decade a housing shortage oppressed the residents of the expanding slums. Smith, who knew the problems of overcrowding at first hand, fought to extend the wartime rent control laws through 1923; this was the least the state could do. He also objected to excessive taxes on real estate which, he understood, would only be passed on to tenants. But he knew from the start that "the only solution" was *more houses*," and that stimulus to new building could only come through the cooperation of government and capital. In 1923 he appointed a committee to lay out a policy for housing and city planning. By the time he left Albany, five years later, he could take credit for a comprehensive housing program that went a long way toward the objective he had sketched out at the start. Under the supervision of a commission, tax exemptions were made available to limited dividend corporations and condemnation procedures made it possible to assemble large tracts for extensive development. Smith did not, however, succeed in persuading the Legislature to create a state land bank to make loans to homeowners.

Apart from rent, the item of the family budget most critical to the poor was that devoted to milk. Immigrants and their children considered milk essential to strength and health. In Europe it had always been a staple of the peasant diet. To deprive a child of his milk was, as it were, to deprive him of his opportunity for the future.

Yet in the city there was no family cow, and milk production was an important part of the state's agriculture. And there was the paradox: while the good women of Oliver Street complained of high prices, the dairymen of Herkimer County bewailed the low returns. The difficulty was clearly between the producer and the consumer, in the distributors. Their greed raised costs, created artificial famines, as during the milk strike of 1919, and even threatened by impurities to poison the children of the state. The explosive character of the issue was revealed when William Randolph Hearst raised it in 1919 and 1926.

Smith tried to bring the representatives of the various parties involved together in conference. But he was hampered all along by the fact that the Department of Farms and Markets was not even responsible to him. There was only one solution, Smith concluded: "The state, through its lawmaking body, must declare the production and distribution of milk to be a public utility, subject to regulation and control by the state itself."

As earlier, the Governor remained aware of the responsibilities of government toward the dependents incapable of protecting themselves. These human resources were as worthy of conservation as the deer and the elk of the forest. On his return to office in 1923 he got the Legislature to reverse an earlier decision that had rejected federal aid for maternity and infancy care. Later he persuaded it also to extend financial support for public health laboratories and nursing services and for county hospitals and health units. A fifty-million-dollar bond issue went to reconstruct state institutions, and he undertook to improve the care for mental defectives.

He went on, furthermore, to advance entirely new proposals. He thus argued that public health stations for infants and mothers should be taken out of "the realm of private philanthropy" and "be fully supported" by the government. He suggested that the state, through rural health centers, subsidize doctors to practice in districts that could afford no other medical service. He asked the Legislature to sponsor a program for health and maternity insurance to protect those hard hit by unexpected expenses and interruptions in their power to earn.

The same concern kept alive his earlier interest in workmen's compensation. Back in 1917 the law had been amended to permit direct settlements between the injured and the insurance companies. That practice was open to many abuses; the agent could "shake the long green before the widow or suffering laborer," who, all too often, was ready to accept any award in preference to extended litigation. Under Smith's sponsorship, new provisions assured workmen a compulsory review by a state referee, shortened the waiting period to seven days, increased the amount of benefits and brought certain occupational diseases within the scope of the insurance. A supplementary measure set up the means for rehabilitating the injured.

Smith tended to take an ever broader view of the definition of dependency. Women held a marginal place in the labor force and needed the special protection of the Bureau of Women in Industry, created in 1919. For years also the Governor argued in favor of a law that would set minimum wages and maximum hours for women, "not as a favor" but "in the interest of the state itself" as a measure in "preservation of public health." Not until 1927, however, did the Legislature enact statutory limits of a forty-eight-hour week for them.

It was also "a matter of state duty" to "conserve our greatest natural resource" by controlling the labor of children. In 1924, at Smith's urging, the law set a fifty-hour week as the maximum for boys between the ages of sixteen and eighteen, and a forty-four-hour week for those between fourteen and sixteen. A year later, however, Smith had already gone farther and advocated ratification of the federal child labor amendment, through which the national government might do what the Supreme Court had forbidden the states to do. Children, he pointed out, were "a national asset and their proper care and early training must be guarded by the Nation."

From this point of view, certainly education demanded adequate support. Time lost here could never be made up. The nation's "future safety" rested on "the school system that will weave into the hearts and minds of generations

to come the principles of American freedom and justice."
When Smith took office, the average salary of New York
teachers was just about one thousand dollars a year.
Shocked, the Governor induced the Legislature to increase
the amount of state aid, particularly to rural schools. With
the advice of an investigating commission, he initiated extensive reforms in the State Board of Education, helped in
the consolidation of small districts, and provided for
more adequate certification as well as for more adequate
salaries for teachers. He also sought special provisions for
adults, for the foreign-born and for working children.
School expenditures went up from nine to eighty million
dollars under his administration. "No other governor,"
a distinguished scholar concluded, "has ever done so much
for public education as Al Smith has."

The broadening experience which permitted him to
deal expertly with these questions also revealed to him
the virtues of some of the changes in government forms
that reformers had long since advanced. He thus came to
see the merit in the idea that the voters be allowed to
propose amendments by initiative. He also advocated the
referendum and urged that it be applied to amendments
to the federal Constitution. He spoke out in favor of
fewer elections, of the short ballot, and of a four-year term
for the governor. He asked similarly that state and national elections be separated so that the issues of one
contest would not influence unduly the outcome of the
other. In 1923, he vetoed a series of changes that threatened to weaken the election law and he urged a tightening
of the corrupt practices act. He thus approached ever more
closely the position formerly occupied by the progressives.

That change reflected a growing awareness, through experience, of the importance of legality and of correct procedures in government. The same respect for the law helped indirectly to shape his attitude toward the Eighteenth Amendment.

His stand in opposition to Prohibition was clear. As governor in 1920 he asked the Legislature to reverse its previous act of ratification; and he remained consistently thereafter in favor of repeal.

Two years later he faced the dilemma of whether or not to approve a bill repealing the Mullan-Gage Act that involved the state in the enforcement of the federal Prohibition Act. No doubt he considered the possibility of evading the question. But finally, at Murphy's urging, he took the Wet side.

In doing so he was not only responsive to the boss. He was also acting in accord with his own deepest convictions. To leave in the statute book a measure that ran counter to the will of the people and that would not be enforced seemed to him to bring the law itself into disrespect. Furthermore, it was not "the function of law to jack up the moral tone of any community." That was "the function of the home and the church." Recognition of the limits of state action was as important as recognition of the capacity of the state to act within those limits. Only thus could the individual be assured of freedom from arbitrary restraint.

At the very start of his gubernatorial career, he had spoken out unequivocally in favor of freedom of speech and of opinion. The Republican Legislature, convinced that the State of New York was "tottering on the verge" of a "Red revolution," enacted "repressive measures of a sort hitherto unheard-of in this country," and barred from their seats a number of duly elected Socialist assem-

blymen. Smith had known some of these men and valued
them as individuals. As president of the Board of Aldermen, he had insisted on treating the Socialist members of
that body as equals. He understood also the unrest that
earned them votes and realized that the "Red scare" was
a threat to every man's liberty. Denouncing the action
of the Legislature, he defended the Socialists and vetoed
the Lusk Bills which would have interfered with freedom
of speech. He continued thereafter to argue against
teachers' loyalty oaths and against movie censorship. He
was for the same reason solicitous of the rights of those
accused of crimes; and, although he was condemned for
doing so, signed the "fence" bill of 1928 that defined
evidence acceptable against receivers of stolen property.

This was a record of which to be proud. Smith had
given the state a vigorous, forceful administration, better
than any it had had in many decades. Strongly pragmatic,
it reflected less a theory of government than a willingness
to apply experience to problems as they arose and a sensi-
tivity to the interests and ideas of the people for whom the
governor acted. Al's achievements strengthened his appeal,
just as his popularity gave him the weapons that enabled
him to act.

In this decade, his reputation had become national.
In 1928, he found himself a symbol of the capacity of
government for progressive action, a refreshing contrast
to the lethargy and self-satisfaction for which Calvin
Coolidge stood. And it seemed to some, although not to
all, Americans that there was an appropriateness to the
identification of progressive action with a person like Al.
In the face of the problems that disturbed modern America, there was hope of a sort in the reflection that the city

streets had been able to produce a man who had risen through his own efforts and had been able decisively to meet every challenge of government.

And he himself, growing in confidence as well as in ability, had already begun to reflect that there was a greater stage still upon which he might play a worthy role.

V I

The Big Prize

Smith never forgot the lines upon which his favorite play closed. How often, as he had played the part of Bardwell Slote, had he listened to the prediction, just before the curtain fell to the crowd's applause, that he would someday be President of the United States!

Of course, that was all acting, and part of the game. The East Side process server and assemblyman, the sheriff of New York County and the president of the Board of Aldermen knew enough to distinguish the play from reality. Still it was tantalizing to think that in the land of opportunity every boy could dream of becoming President. And in 1918 the man who had been the boy, Al, had already seen many dreams surprisingly become true.

But it was another matter for the governor of the State of New York to have such dreams. By 1918, the chief executive of a large state stood in a crucial relationship to the Presidency.

Down through the Civil War, the candidacy for the country's highest office had generally gone to men who had won national prominence through service either in

Congress, the Cabinet or the Army. It seemed reasonable to select for the race a man whose name was thus widely known. Toward the end of the nineteenth century, however, other factors altered the calculation. The nomination itself became a prize to be struggled for, and the arena of the contest was the national convention, a body that became larger and larger with the growth of population.

In a convention organized by states, the governors carried enormous weight. A senator or secretary of state might have prestige, but he usually controlled no delegates. The state organization chose the members of the convention; and any governor with ability could marshal his delegation in a tight formation that followed his lead and served his interests. In the party which controlled the national administration, the President had some resources with which to offset those of the governors. In the party out of office in Washington, power like patronage flowed out of the Governor's Mansion.

New York was the nation's largest state: in the Democratic National Convention it disposed of by far the most important single bloc of votes. Its governor was almost automatically a prospective candidate for the presidential nomination and was, Al pointed out, usually to be found "sitting on the steps of the capitol at Albany with his spyglass trained on Washington." These considerations were certainly familiar to Smith in 1919; and although his attention was focused upon the administration of the state, his mind could not fail to turn to wider possibilities. Politics itself was a game, and, as in all games, chance played its part. The turn of the play had brought the biggest prize of all within reach. Having come so far, why should he not go farther? In the 1920 convention at San Francisco he received a noteworthy ovation and earned a few token votes. That was not serious. But it might be a sign significant for the future. Somewhere in the early years of the governorship that thought became a goad to action.

A rigorous code of etiquette regulated the behavior of potential Democratic candidates. Men ambitious to be nominated and elected had to conform to the peculiar conditions of the party situation.

There was just one thing wrong with the party; it didn't have enough votes. A minority in the nation and internally divided, it had won a presidential election under only two leaders since 1856. It could do so again only if it were united. A nomination gained at the cost of ir-reparable splits within the party was valueless. William Jennings Bryan had learned that lesson three times over.

Yet the party was, in fact, made up of diverse elements, and the divisions among them were real and not to be blinked away. Two-thirds rule recognized those differences by giving a minority the power to block an unacceptable choice. Each faction sought its own ends and if it were defeated in the selection of a candidate, it had somehow to be pacified, lest it bolt or fail to bring out the vote on election day.

The divisions within the party followed no simple orderly pattern. Old sectional lines separated Northerners from Southerners and Westerners from Easterners. But there were also confusing social differences of great sig-nificance between the conservative descendants of the Bourbons of the 1880's and a rather radical wing which had once flirted with Populism and the Progressives. Again. the representatives of the city machines sat uncomfortably in the same hall with rural and small-town folk, who regarded them as suspiciously foreign.

Under these conditions, the period between conventions was one of strategic maneuver, in which a variety of cliques shifted and re-formed in alliances in preparation for the tactical struggles of the convention itself.

The greatest danger was to be an open candidate too soon. Nothing brought the diverse blocs together more effectively than a common enemy. The front runner was a threat to the interests of every hopeful and could ordinarily expect to see them unite to bring him down before they turned to arrangements of their own. It was by far the safer procedure to make a pretense of disinterestedness while laying a groundwork for future support and to be available when the convention began to compromise its differences.

These problems of maneuver were particularly important for the city machines, and most important of all for Tammany. Of all elements in the party, they occupied the least advantageous position when it came to the formation of alliances. For years, Tammany had been a convenient symbol used by ambitious Easterners to capture rural Southern and Western votes. Grover Cleveland and Woodrow Wilson had thus ingratiated themselves with many delegates by their attacks on the New York County organization. They had proved that in the convention at large it sometimes was better to be an enemy than a friend of Tammany. When Cox in 1920 consulted Murphy with regard to the Vice-Presidency, Silent Charlie said in amazement: "This is the first time a Democratic nominee for the Presidency has shown me courtesy. That's why I would vote for the devil himself if Cox wanted me to."

To counteract the usual latent hostility it was necessary to move cautiously, and only from positions of proved strength. That consideration dominated Smith's strategy down to the convention of 1924.

Smith began with the advantages as well as with the liabilities of Tammany support. With some confusion and with some ambiguity of attitude, Murphy and his followers began to understand that one of their boys had a chance for the White House. However they may have felt about Smith's role in the state, they had no alternative but to support him without reservation for the Presidency. He was, after all, one of their own; and wouldn't it be quite a thing to have an Irish Catholic from the East Side running the country? Besides, then, it might not be too bad to have Al off in Washington, occupied with important matters, while a somewhat less austere Democratic governor took over in Albany. And, when one got right down to it, Smith had so much power in the machine in his own right, that it would be foolhardy not to back him up. The Hall would do what it could.

The campaign began slowly and cautiously under the general advice of Joseph Proskauer, during Smith's second administration. In 1923, it involved mostly a careful process of establishing connections outside the state and preparing for the eventualities of the 1924 convention.

The Smith forces, under George Brennan of Illinois and Norman Mack of Buffalo, approached that gathering with no feeling of certainty that they could have the nomination, but also with no feeling that it was essential to win then. Their candidate was young and could afford to wait another four years. They were encouraged by favorable returns from the Wisconsin and Minnesota primaries. But for the time being only a strong showing was important, one which would make Al favorably known to the nation and leave him in an advantageous position for the future. If there were any chance of immediate success, they would of course seize it. But the ability to hold off was a distinct tactical asset, as was the fact that the convention would be held in Madison Square Garden, on home ground in New York.

Yet by the time the gavel of the temporary chairman descended, Smith had been compelled to take account of a taboo which he had known existed, but which he had refused to recognize. Now a confrontation with "the religious tradition which has hitherto prevented the nomination of a Catholic for President" was unavoidable and that altered the whole strategy of the campaign.

Smith's career had been a demonstration of the validity of Americanism. In his own mind, his success had confirmed the premise established by his life on the East Side, by his career in the Assembly, and by his election to the governorship — that men of diverse backgrounds and different beliefs could nevertheless understand one another and work together toward common objectives. Opportunity beckoned to all; it was unthinkable that anyone should be held back because of the peculiarities of his origins or the distinctiveness of his beliefs.

Yet, disturbingly, at this very time, some Americans were questioning that basic assumption.

It had begun earlier in the century, in the movement to restrict immigration, when the enemies of the foreign-born had developed the argument that some peoples were racially inferior to others. The newcomers from Southern and Eastern Europe, it was said, were innately unequal to those from the North and the West. During the war, prejudice had gained force from ugly manifestations of intolerance and hostility to everything alien. The shock of sudden entry into the great conflict evoked among some Americans a patriotism different from that in which Smith had faith, one of total conformity and 100 per cent Americanism rather than one that found its strength in diversity. Al had scarcely comprehended the force of these emotions; to him these were the wild eccentricities of a few extremists.

In the postwar period, however, intolerance did not subside, but actually spread with disquieting speed. In the mood of disillusion and apparent betrayal engendered by the unsuccessful peace, many Americans longed to believe that somehow the fault had not been in themselves but in external force. They sought safety in withdrawal, in rejection of the League of Nations, in the destruction of Wilson's handiwork, in the end of immigration, and in security through isolation. International ties of every sort were dangerous; there was a hidden threat in the connections of Catholics and Jews with the outer world.

These fears revived the Ku Klux Klan. Founded in 1915 in Georgia, the organization was still small and powerless at the end of the war. Thereafter it spread rapidly, not only in the South but everywhere in rural and small-town America. It was particularly influential in Oregon and Indiana and had significant centers of strength throughout the West.

The masked men — perhaps four million of them — who secretly assembled on the hillsides under the fiery crosses were afraid of the new world their country had become. Science had abolished the God of their fathers;

strange influences emanating from the city had weakened the family and had destroyed traditional standards of authority; intemperance created bad habits; and corruption spread through politics and business.

Yes, everybody was doing it. But was it right? Across the night the faceless men saw the big cars slide up to the roadhouse, heard the couples jazz it up in the country club. In town, the lurid movie posters drew the boys and girls to the worship of foreign stars whose names glittered across the headlines. Everyone was doing it, dissolving in the haze of the good time and the big money; and they themselves knew the urgency of repression because they themselves felt the urging toward it. NOBODY SHOULD DO IT. Only thus could anybody be safe.

Purification was essential through a return to the old order, through fundamentalism in religion, through abstinence and restraint in personal behavior, and through the forceful excision from the government and the economy of all alien sources of infection.

Unhappily, the old order had never existed except in the wishful dreams of men unwilling to confront the future. For three centuries, the American soil had been hostile to tradition and authority; there was no consolation in looking back to the precedents of the real past and history therefore was bunk as Henry Ford proclaimed. Nor was there profit in examining the actualities of corruption in the present; it would have been hard to find any but old-stock names among those who created the scandals of the Harding administration.

But reality had nothing to do with it in the minds of those who conjured up the threatening images of the international Jew and the international Catholic. (The

Negro was distinctly a lesser danger to the Klansmen of the 1920's.) The millions of adherents of the Roman Church, held in subservience to a foreign despot by an army of priests and bishops, wielded enormous political power through the city machines. Their doctrines and rituals, like their hostility to Prohibition, were a danger to the old America. It was necessary to prepare lest they insidiously assume control of the whole nation. So ran the leaflets and the fiery speeches.

Smith did not take the Klan seriously, even in 1924. As late as May of that year, he saw no reason for alarm. The "spirit of unrest" was an "unnatural consequence of war" and would soon subside. The idea that sober men might be swept away by such slogans was so alien to his experience that he could not believe it true. The Klan was "so abhorrent to intelligent thinking Americans of all denominations, that it must in time fall to the ground of its own weight. The Catholics of the country can stand it. The Jews can stand it. But the United States of America cannot stand it."

The Klan, which had theretofore shown itself mostly on the local level, was nonetheless to be the pre-eminent issue of the 1924 convention. Much of the strength of the organization was located in the Republican Party, which was able to arrive at a tacit decision to evade any mention of the Klan in the campaign. But the order was also securely anchored in the Southern and Western branches of the Democratic Party, which was not so fortunately situated. When the delegates assembled in Madison Square Garden the Northeastern groups representing urban, immigrant constituencies confronted the rural Southerners and Westerners. The former wanted some explicit condemnation of the Ku Klux Klan, the latter preferred to emulate the silence of the G.O.P.

The Committee on Resolutions that had met two days earlier at the Waldorf had split wide open on the question. The majority proposed a vague and innocuous plank calculated to soothe the sensibilities of the Klansmen. The minority was determined to bring the issue of intolerance out into the open and resolved to carry the fight onto the floor of the Garden.

By the time the convention was organized and prepared to vote on the platform on the night of June 29, 1924, tempers were at fever pitch. An ugly mood spread among the delegates, who squirmed with the heat of the debate as well as with that of the sultry evening. The final vote, 546.15 for the Klan and 542.85 against it, left everyone angry and resentful.

The bitterness affected the choice of a nominee. There was after all no more important issue than that of the character of Americanism; and men who divided on that were not likely to unite on anything else.

The leading candidate was William G. McAdoo of California, Wilson's son-in-law and heir apparent to his position. McAdoo had served as Secretary of the Treasury, had a strong national reputation, and enjoyed many connections within the party. He was known as a liberal, although his services as attorney for the Doheny oil interests had cooled the ardor of some of his followers. It would, obviously, be more difficult to capitalize upon Republican corruption in the Teapot Dome affair if he were the Democratic standard-bearer. Still McAdoo had a majority — although not the requisite two-thirds — of the delegates in his camp when the convention met.

Smith had not been favorably disposed to McAdoo to begin with. Back in 1920 he had resented the Californian's uncompromising Dry position and had then helped block his nomination. Al had looked for some signs of a reaction to the question of the Klan; but McAdoo adamantly refused to take any position whatever and his supporters, William Jennings Bryan among them, were in the forefront of those who had fought against tolerance. Now the forces were clearly ranged: on one side the fanaticism of the Klan, of Prohibition, and of fundamentalism; on the other, the hope of an America that still meant liberty and equality of opportunity. Now there could be no compromise. McAdoo had to be defeated and the issue had to be tested. Could any man become President? Could a Catholic be nominated?

While the bands played "The Sidewalks of New York," Smith grimly watched the course of the balloting. The vote on the platform had already shown that he himself had no chance. But he was staying in the race to punish the man who would not declare himself. By the third ballot, it was clear that the convention was in a deadlock; yet the delegates were doomed to move through one weary tally after another. There was no means of resolving the conflict. This was a showdown. Everybody knew it.

At one interval among the endless roll calls, William Jennings Bryan rose to speak — now sixty-four years old and no longer the boy orator. His balding head, fringed by a graying halo of hair, shone under the lights like a torch of the righteousness of which he spoke. A year later, in Dayton, Tennessee, he would sink into a ridiculous morass as he defended his fundamentalist God against evolution; he could not stand it not to be taken seriously and would die of chagrin. Now he had taken time off from his speculation in Florida real estate to act the elder statesman.

Bryan was as welcome in New York "as a safety-razor manufacturer at a barbers' convention." As the spectators recognized him, they burst into unrestrained hissing and booing. Defiantly the old man looked up at the galleries and flung the challenge back at them. "You do not represent the future of our country." That was the question: who did?

The Western Catholics who supported McAdoo desperately sought some compromise. They suggested that Al throw his support to a Dry Catholic like Senator Walsh of Montana. In return for an immediate withdrawal, they offered to arrange a deal whereby Smith would be assured the nomination in 1928. Smith would make no deals, and McAdoo was equally determined not to compromise.

Not until after one hundred ballots did Al yield and then only on condition that all the candidates release their delegates and permit the convention to make a free choice. On the hundred and third ballot, John W. Davis received a weary and unenthusiastic nomination.

The dark horse found his victory worthless. The convention itself had all but ruined his chances; and he was obliged to bear the further handicap of a weak running mate. Charles W. Bryan, the Vice-Presidential candidate, was a brother of William Jennings, who had already distinguished himself in opposition to Smith. Many liberal-minded voters deserted to La Follette, the third party candidate, while the conservatives were content with Coolidge. More important, apathy and disgust kept many at home; only 50 per cent of those eligible went to the polls in 1924.

Smith campaigned valiantly for Davis, whom he respected. But the cause was hopeless. At the canvass, the Democratic vote stood at little more than eight million, while the Republican was well above fifteen.

Perhaps nothing could have helped in the face of Coolidge prosperity. But the outcome of the convention had certainly alienated many Democrats in the Northeastern cities. The question was often asked, for instance, whether it was possible to vote for Davis without voting for Bryan. And there was clear-cut testimony of the effect in the fact that Smith, "the eighth wonder of the world," who carried New York in the gubernatorial race, ran almost one million votes ahead of his ticket.

The results were felt long thereafter. Advancing age, his role in the convention and his failure to work for Davis put an end to McAdoo's active career. Influential supporters like Bernard M. Baruch and Thomas L. Chadbourne, a distinguished liberal lawyer, now deserted him. For Smith, on the other hand, there was consolation in the thought that probably no Democrat could have beaten Coolidge in 1924 and satisfaction in the success of his campaign for re-election. "Governor Smith emerges from the Democratic wreck a bigger figure than ever before," proclaimed the Newark *News*. The defeat of Hylan and Hearst in New York City a year later added still further to Al's stature.

Nevertheless, through the busy period of preoccupation with the affairs of New York State, Smith could not forget what had happened in Madison Square Garden. Deep within there remained the determination to prove that the bigotry displayed in the convention was not representative of the true feelings of the American people. This was more important than any specific question of government policy.

In the four years before 1928 Smith's situation improved perceptibly. Al grew in stature as he triumphed again in the state election of 1926 and as his administration continued to attract attention throughout the country. Thomas L. Chadbourne was one of a group that set to work making the Governor nationally known. Joseph P. Tumulty, Wilson's secretary, also worked behind the scenes toward the same end. Meanwhile, the Klan collapsed in the face of scandals that put its leaders behind prison bars. Some of the obstacles in the way of Smith's nomination thus disappeared.

At the same time, the old rifts were healed or, more properly speaking, were patched over. By the shock of Madison Square Garden, the party seemed to have gotten Bryanism out of its system. The Democratic leaders realized how serious had been the divisions of 1924 and they were resolved to avoid a repetition. As Mark Sullivan pointed out, the failure to nominate Smith "would be an act so calling for explanation as to weaken them in the country." Furthermore, the Democrats knew they could not win without New York; and Smith alone seemed capable of carrying the Empire State.

Hidden resentments, it was true, remained. Josephus Daniels and other Southerners warned that a wave of hatred would follow the selection of Smith as the candidate; and certain Western Catholics like Thomas J. Walsh of Montana and Arthur F. Mullen of Nebraska feared to have the religious issue raised once more. Above all, the dark secret prejudice against the urban foreigner was still nurtured by fear and desire. "If you think this country ain't Dry," Will Rogers warned, "you just watch 'em vote; and if you think this country ain't Wet, you just watch 'em drink. You see, when they vote, it's counted; but when they drink, it ain't. If you could register the man's breath that cast the ballots, that would be great. But the voting strength of this country is Dry."

Of these subterranean emotions Smith was not at all aware. He had the city man's exaggerated faith in his country cousin's straightforward innocence. Rubes though some of them might be, people everywhere were all God's children and all basically alike. Deacon Tillinger — the avaricious religious hypocrite of John Golden's *Turn to the Right* — always went down to defeat before the forces of goodness in the village. Al had not been much in the South, but wasn't it all familiar: the showboat tied by the levee, the folks singing "Swanee" or "Dixie" while the darkies hummed the blues, and sweet Georgia Brown in a mist of magnolia, while chivalry shone through the colonnade? And the West, where men were men and no one asked your name, for it was what you were that counted, on the prairie where Buffalo Bill strode his mount and everywhere was the loyalty of *My Partner* . . . Ah, how could the man know that all these images had been made on his own Broadway and had nothing to do with Senator Heflin's Alabama or Senator Owen's Oklahoma? Al was sure to get the nomination, but little joy it would bring him.

As a concession to Southern sensibilities and to Jesse Jones, the convention was held in Houston; and it had to be stretched out for six days to bring the guarantors out of the red. Enthusiastic delegations made the trip from the Northeastern cities to participate in the "event of a lifetime." But by contrast with 1924, the sessions were rather dull; "it was the longest wake any Irishman ever attended," was the comment of one of the participants.

The Smith forces had been carefully organized, and substantial strength was mobilized well in advance. Franklin Roosevelt, eminently respectable and not identified either with Tammany or with the Wets, acted as floor leader. After the favorite sons had made their showing and had been eliminated, Al was handily nominated. In a show of unity the Vice-Presidential place, about which Smith himself had no strong feelings, went to Joseph Robinson, a Southerner and a moderate Dry.

There was a widespread consciousness that Prohibition would be a touchy issue. The platform attempted to equivocate by pledging the party to support the law. Apart from that, the statement of policy was clear and forthright — in favor of aid to the farmers and workers, of collective bargaining, of the abolition of labor injunctions, and of the stricter regulation of power companies.

Prospects for success in November were hardly bright; but they were not hopeless. The Republican candidate, Secretary of Commerce Herbert C. Hoover, did not arouse the enthusiasm of the rank and file of his own party. He was suspect, having once been a Democrat, and seemed to have secured the nomination largely for want of an alternative and through the indecision of President Coolidge. There was a chance at least of victory.

Smith's campaign organization developed rapidly and effectively. His friend Kenny and Ed Flynn of the Bronx had recently introduced him to a vice-president of General Motors who would play an important part in his life in the next few years. John Jacob Raskob was another poor boy who had come up in the world. Born in Lockport. New York, in 1879, the son of an Alsatian father and an

Irish mother, he had knocked around from one job to another and had then come to work as secretary for Pierre S. Du Pont. In 1914, while the affairs of William C. Durant's automobile empire were in disorder, he and Du Pont had privately bought some stock in it. Four years later he persuaded the Du Ponts to acquire a controlling share. Thereafter, Raskob was prominent in the affairs of General Motors. A born salesman, he had sponsored the scheme of installment buying that did much to put the firm in the forefront of the industry.

In 1928, he was approaching fifty and independently wealthy. He had taken little interest in politics. But he was a devout Catholic, the father of twelve children, and he had been disturbed by the Klan and the episode of 1924, particularly since he had spent so much time in the free-and-easy atmosphere of Detroit where religious prejudice seemed altogether out of place. Introduced to Smith one evening in Kenny's Tiger Room, he was impressed with the Governor's ability and charm. Certainly it would be a proud thing, for America and for the Church, to demonstrate that Catholicism was at home in the United States by putting Al in the White House.

Smith in turn was taken with Raskob, the kind of self-made successful man he admired. The two hit it off well together; and Al asked his new friend to become chairman of the Democratic National Committee. He paid no attention to those among his advisers who warned him against the elevation of Catholics to places of prominence. He would have nothing to do with such timid compromises. Raskob gave up his position in General Motors and lavishly devoted his time and money to the cause of Smith's election.

Al's personal campaign was directed by Belle Moskowitz. He drew upon the services of a large staff of dedicated volunteers and had the assistance of a brain trust guided by Professor Lindsay Rogers of Columbia University. Carefully planned speeches, delivered throughout the country, thoughtfully attacked the important issues, including that of agriculture, and made his position known. By now a seasoned campaigner, he put to their most critical test the techniques he had developed since 1918 in New York.

They failed. Although Smith's popular vote almost doubled that of Davis in 1924, Hoover was the victor by a resounding plurality. Most dismaying of all, Al failed to carry his own state and lost also sectors of the Solid South that had been loyal to the Democratic Party since reconstruction.

There was no single cause for the defeat.

Smith had, of course, to struggle against the currents of complacency set up by the wild prosperity of 1928. Less than a year later the country would pay dearly for its heedlessness. But for the moment, the prevailing optimism and the material well-being of the nation made it difficult to carry on a critical campaign.

Furthermore, Smith proved inflexible in his unwillingness to pander to the mood of the times. This was not simply the result of his lack of familiarity with the country outside New York. His advisers and he knew what was expected of him; and, dealing with some kinds of problems, as with the farm question in his Omaha speech, he proved surprisingly effective. But upon other matters he would not compromise in the slightest. He insisted on being taken as he was, out of a profound, if naïve, faith that his honesty and integrity would get across to this widest audience of all.

Thus he refused to hedge when Hoover charged that Smith was taking a road to Socialism. In his reply in Boston, Al reaffirmed his conviction of the importance of his program and pointed out that the accusation of Communism was always an easy weapon in the hands of the enemies of progressive legislation.

So too he refused to soften his stand on Prohibition. Dissatisfied with the party platform, he sent a telegram to the convention making his own repeal position clear. To the reporters he made a rigorous, candid statement that was "a political classic." Thereafter he was the victim of a vicious whispering campaign that circulated slanderous rumors of his drunkenness among the horrified ladies of the W.C.T.U.

Most important of all, he refused to pretend that he was not what he was — a Catholic, a grandson of Irish immigrants, a poor boy from off the sidewalks of New York. Let it be a test, he thought, of whether such a one as he could be President. Bitterly, he resented the jokes as to what a figure his wife would make in the White House. When a photographer asked her to take off some jewelry for a picture, Al angrily burst out, "Leave Katie alone!" In his eyes, she was as worthy as anyone to be first lady of the land.

By the same token, he refused to conceal the evidences of his New York origins. He could say "radio" and "hospital" with the best of them in Iowa or Virginia. But despite well-intentioned advice from his entourage he insisted on saying "rad-dio" and "horspital." It was as if he feared that in concealing the accents of the Bowery he would be turning his back upon the people among whom he had grown up, be untrue to himself and to them. No amount of votes was worth it.

Openly and squarely he faced the religious issue. The Klan was dead. But anti-Catholicism was alive. Even at the convention there had been a backstairs undertow about Al Smith's religion. But his enemies, realizing they could not keep the nomination from him, dedicated themselves to making it a worthless thing in the election. A vicious campaign attacked the Church and painted a horrendous picture of the downfall of free institutions at the hands of the priests whose tool Smith was. With the covert encouragement of local Republicans, numerous fundamentalist groups spread the tale of the Papist plot to conquer America at the ballot box.

Smith had dealt with the question reasonably in the exchange of articles in the *Atlantic Monthly*. He had then assumed that the doubts of Protestants were expressed in good faith; and he attempted logically and calmly to show that Catholics faced no conflict of loyalties between their religious and political obligations. The "conscience of the individual" was the ultimate guide to action; and so long as the individual was free to act in accordance with the dictates of his conscience, the nation had nothing to fear. But logic was a poor instrument to stem the tide of hatred set loose in the campaign. As the weeks went by, the Democratic candidate recognized that prejudice influenced not a few eccentrics only but a large part of his countrymen.

Al made no pretense that the problem did not exist. In North Carolina he insisted on speaking on immigration. In Oklahoma City, one of the centers of Klan strength, he launched into an attack upon the forces injecting bigotry "into a campaign which should be an intelligent debate of the important issues." He had prepared this speech with care, a good speech and persuasive to the friends for whom he had rehearsed it. But now as he looked down upon the stony faces, row upon row of bitter farmers soon to leave their parched lands, he perceived the dull hostility in their staring at his strangeness and for a moment he felt a premonitory fear, for what had he and they in common? But then he thought he must rouse these people from their prejudices. Here and now, he declared desperately, I "drag them into the open and I denounce them as a treasonable attack upon the very foundations of American liberty. I have been told that politically it might be expedient for me to remain silent upon this subject, but as far as I am concerned no political expediency will keep me from speaking out in an endeavor to destroy these evil attacks."

In 1928, candor and the plea for tolerance did not help. The farmer and the small-town merchant, the fundamentalist and the prohibitionist, blinded by fear of the future, struck out in fury against the urban stranger who was the symbol of the new America.

Through the rimless glasses across his thin parched face, Bishop Cannon had looked bitterly out upon the Houston convention. Control had fallen to the men from "the foreign-populated city called New York" where "confessedly Satan's seat is." Once he had thought the greatest question before the nation was the "translation into the social order of the teaching of Jesus Christ concerning human brotherhood"; and he had appealed to the industrial leaders of the South for social justice. Now, although still professing his freedom from bigotry, he was resolved that "no subject of the Pope" should be President. Any means were justified in safeguarding Prohibition, the "high-water mark attained by the American people to promote the general welfare."

An inner uneasiness gnawed at his conscience as he moved through the Southern back country in a campaign of reckless invective against Al Smith. The images still lingered of the days when he had gone down as a student at the Princeton Seminary to look at the "publicans, harlots and sinners" of the Bowery. He was tormented also with the anxieties of secret speculation on the stock market; it was a strain to justify to himself this use of funds entrusted to him for another purpose. And other strains, less readily eased, added to the passion with which he spoke of the effects of alcohol on "sexual nature." He was not to be at peace with himself even two years later when, his invalid wife having died, he married his secretary at the age of sixty-six.

The Bishop's torment was symptomatic of the disturbed emotions of many citizens who now turned against the Democratic candidate. With William Allen White, their spokesman, they attacked Smith as the representative of the "saloon, prostitution, and gambling," as the spokesman of "a group who have back of them only physical appetite and no regard for law or reform." In maudlin self-pity they bewailed the loss of what had never been — oh, those good old days when "our national policies were such policies as an intelligent, upright, altruistic American farmer might formulate in an eminently respectable world in which each man earned all he got and in which every man got all he earned." Yes, then "we were of one blood as we were of one tongue," and it was "English blood, or

Teutonic blood if you will" which "naturally takes to agriculture." So different *he,* and hateful in his difference.
Better to take a Republican than a Wet, a Catholic and a
foreigner, even in the South, which had reached the dead
end of its ancient dreams. Scores of Democratic politicians
failed to support or secretly opposed their own candidate.

Smith did make gains, hidden for the moment by the
magnitude of the defeat, but immensely significant for the
future. He carried Massachusetts, for instance, the first
time a Democrat had done so since the Civil War. That
was an indication of the awakening of a great army of
immigrant voters in all the big cities — French Canadian,
Italian and Jewish, as well as Irish — who would long
thereafter be lost to the G.O.P. In the South, Hoover had
supported the lily-white Republicans and thereby alienated
many Negroes who voted for Smith. That transfer of
allegiance would continue for the next two decades.

Smith had also earned the support of a smaller band of
thoughtful Americans like John Dewey and George W.
Norris because "his undeniable virtue" made clear an issue
that had long been blurred. For Ellery Sedgwick, Al was
the "sign and symbol of a great change." He spoke "for
millions who have not learned all our ways; and why should
they, when we will learn none of theirs." But the nation's
rural past was ended and it was pre-eminently important
not to "fool our own souls by voting before the world for
a secret reason which the more decent of us dare scarcely
even murmur to themselves."

On election night, Smith sat in the Seventy-first Regi-
ment Armory as the returns came in. At 9:30 o'clock he
knew the result. The unlighted cigar clamped in his teeth

drooped slightly and he prepared to go home, taking the outcome gallantly and calmly. He had clung to every shred of hope as long as possible, although, as a serious politician, he had already recognized the signs of what was to come.

What distressed him most was not defeat, but the manner of it; and particularly, the defection of those Democrats moved purely by bigotry and prejudice. The big prize had escaped him; but a man learned to take the bad with the good. Only it was disturbing to be forced to wonder whether his conception of Americanism was at fault. Could it be that he had not read aright the lesson of his own life? If Americans were not really willing to accept an Irish Catholic as fully their equal, where then did he belong?

In 1925, another grandson of an Irish immigrant had told the story of a tragic failure to win a big prize. The hero of that story was a stranger led on by an incorruptible dream. Great in his ability to seize all the lesser rewards of life, he met disaster when he reached out for that which would have made his life worth living. Gatsby's fault lay not in himself but in the dream that led him to accept without qualification the values of those who belonged but who had themselves lost faith. Adherence to their ideals — which no longer held them — doomed him to betrayal; and both the dream and the manner of its frustration were symbolic of the New World's opportunities for achievement and for tragedy.

A year and a half after his defeat, in an article for a popular magazine, Smith recalled a favorite oration: Richard L. Shiel's reply, in the House of Commons, to the accusation that the Irish were "aliens in race, aliens in country and aliens in religion." Al quoted from the speech his favorite lines, which he had often delivered as a youth: "Partakers in every peril, in the glory are we not to be permitted to participate? And shall we be told as a requital that we are estranged from the whole country for whose salvation our lifeblood was poured out?"

The fears evoked by those poignant queries would continue to bother Al Smith through the rest of his life; and their impact would be the deeper because there was no one to whom they could be expressed. Politics, one of his friends had warned him, was the only sport in the world where they didn't pay off for second money. To run second in any other event was an honor; to run second for the Presidency was just a pity.

In the years after 1928, Al would be for the first time in his life without an audience; and, oh, it was hard to find something to say when no one was listening.

V I I

The Outsiders

ANOTHER MAN had listened to the returns on election night of 1928. He too had heard the news of the disaster with dismay — a dismay heightened by his sense of personal loss.

Through the early evening, his friends noticed that Franklin D. Roosevelt seemed mostly occupied with the race for the Presidency. But as the results took form, his thoughts focused upon his chances in the gubernatorial contest. The early totals were not encouraging. He ran behind Smith in the Democratic cities; and perhaps his mind already phrased the terms in which he would concede.

As the night advanced, however, his prospects improved. The returns from the normally Republican rural districts were bringing him ahead. When he went to bed, there was a chance; in the morning, he learned that he had carried the governorship, although Smith had lost the presidential vote of New York State.

The next few weeks then were time for stocktaking. The surprising outcome of the election had upset a carefully balanced timetable; and Roosevelt was resilient enough to take advantage af the opportunities and to avoid the dangers of the situation.

The past decade had been one of continuing disappointment to the man whose career had started brilliantly and rapidly. He had left Harvard twenty years earlier with a determination to make his way in politics; and his earliest efforts had been singularly successful. In 1910, he had gained genuine prominence in the state Senate; and then had moved to the national scene when he became Undersecretary of the Navy in Wilson's administration. In 1920, the necessities of balancing the ticket and the magic of the Roosevelt name had made the young man Democratic Vice-Presidential candidate. Until then, he had hardly known Smith; and indeed had opposed Al's gubernatorial nomination in 1918.

However, defeat in 1920 and a tragic illness had seemed to put an end to Roosevelt's political career. In the next few years, he was incapable of being a candidate or of holding any office. But he had come to know Smith better and had developed a sincere admiration for his qualities as governor. In 1924 Roosevelt, so valiant in his recovery, had made the nominating speech for the Happy Warrior and in 1928 had been his floor manager in Houston.

But a tinge of mutual resentment had always kept the two men from genuine intimacy. Roosevelt's patrician upbringing — at Hyde Park, in Groton, and in Harvard — had left him with an ambition for achievement and with a sense of *noblesse oblige* in the direction of public service. In both respects Tammany had initially been an obstacle. By 1920, however, he had learned a good deal about the rough-and-tumble of politics and in his own fashion thereafter became a consummate politician. But he never comfortably assimilated the code of the gang; loyalty to the organization and its leader and the obligation, within the group, to deal straight from the top of the deck were nurtured by kinds of personal relationships he did not altogether understand.

Roosevelt too had been brought up in an atmosphere that stressed the compulsion to understatement. This was the means by which old families like his own separated themselves from the *nouveaux riches.* Between themselves and the outlanders they interposed a bland wall of good taste and decorum that kept apart the vulgar exhibitionism of the lavish spenders. It was not that any particular virtue inhered in thrift as such. But to keep familiar furniture in a familiar house, to wear the same old hat indefinitely, to buy a dollar-ninety-eight shirt, to eat scrambled eggs as a traditional Sunday night supper and to wash that down with milk or good cold water was to affirm a standard of values independent of, and superior to, that of money. It kept a man apart from, and above, the kind of people who redecorated their apartments annually, who pursued fashion in clothes and who frequented the famous restaurants and speakeasies. These standards had been made a part of Franklin Roosevelt from his youth; and if he was ever tempted to forget them, his mother and wife were there to remind him of them.

The trouble was, he was often tempted. He was a man of good humor and robust tastes and now and then slipped down the road to his friend's for the drink he could not have at home. But generally he conformed to the restraints his position dictated.

It was inevitable that he should feel awkward in Smith's suite at the Biltmore. All those people! He may never actually have dined at the Tiger Room, but he must have heard stories of the goings-on. He could not, without denying his own background, fail to disapprove of the kinds of people Al and his friends were. When Smith came to visit at his mother's, Franklin like Eleanor noticed the "little barbs" Sarah Roosevelt directed against the East Sider.

And yet mingled with the disapproval was a touch of envy at being left out of the fun. Never one of the boys, Franklin Roosevelt felt cut off from the good humor and high spirits of the group and sometimes, almost wistfully, stopped by for Robert Moses, on the chance that they might go down to the Governor's together.

In these years, of course, Al came to know somewhat better the young senator whom he had met back in Albany, whom he had helped nominate in 1920, and who now moved around the outskirts of his own circle. It was useful to have Roosevelt in the entourage — an Anglo-Saxon, Protestant, good family, good name. He was hardly to be taken seriously as a political force, however. He had, after all, never been elected to anything outside Dutchess County. Still, he had made a gallant fight against his crippling illness; he had made a dramatic appearance in Madison Square Garden in 1924 after he had been told what to say; and he was a hard and willing worker. Smith had been anxious to have him run for the governorship in 1928; and had personally asked him to do so to strengthen the ticket.

That was not a sign so much of confidence in Roosevelt the man as of the usefulness of his name. To Smith, in

1928, Roosevelt remained a pleasant, rich man's son, who had never worked and who had never had to prove himself by coming up in the world as Al and his friends had. Furthermore, an East Sider had his own conception of manners; and Sarah Roosevelt's little barbs scarcely went unnoticed. Indeed, Al may have been sensitive to more slights than were intended — not that it made much difference to him what a tony Harvard thought. He never suspected that, beneath the other man's aloofness, there was a hidden longing to be taken in. And Roosevelt, who could read in Al's attitude a patronizing dismissal of his own lack of achievement, set it down to an inverted snobbishness of the newly arrived against the well-established; and that, hardening his own sense of reserve, only cut him further off from the Smith group he did not know how to approach.

So that even in 1928, while they worked closely with one another in a common enterprise, the two men were outsiders to each other. Misunderstandings arose as when, in the interval between the convention and the election, Roosevelt thought he was being denied access to the Governor. The differences between them were not on matters of policy or interest, but purely personal, the products of their dissimilar backgrounds. For that very reason, those differences were not recognized; and, unrecognized, they festered. They would be prolonged, with unfortunate consequences, on into the next decade.

The situation became clearer to Roosevelt than it did to Smith. The new governor had not only ambitions but a timetable. His ultimate destination was the White House, and Albany was the way to it as it had been for his cousin Theodore Roosevelt. He and his devoted aide, Louis Howe, had planned to aim for the governorship in 1932 in order to be in a position to strike for the Presidency in 1936. They acceded to Smith's pleas and made the race in 1928 with genuine reluctance.

The results upset their calculations. The chief executive of New York State was almost automatically a presidential candidate; when Roosevelt arrived in Warm Springs a few days after the election he was already hailed as such by Southerners. At once he perceived two imperatives: he must establish his reputation as governor; and he must look ahead to the nomination in 1932.

In both respects Smith was an obstacle. The brilliant reputation of Al's administration threatened to overshadow anything his successor might do. Roosevelt knew he would have to strike out on his own lest he be regarded as only the tail of Smith's kite.

Furthermore, it was essential to bypass Smith in order to get at the presidential nomination. Whether Al intended to try again or not was irrelevant. Roosevelt could only win if he came into the convention with substantial support from his own state and from delegates elsewhere.

The strategy of the next four years was clear. It would be difficult to draw away Smith's friends, although something might be done through adroit political maneuver. But the primary effort would have to be to win Al's enemies, the diehard Southerners and the rural voters everywhere. Aware that Smith would continue to be powerful in the cities, Roosevelt acutely perceived the necessity of emphasizing traditional policies to attract traditional votes — to play down Prohibition and the religious issue, to avoid antagonizing either the Tammany or the anti-Tammany forces, to emphasize aid to agriculture and tariff reform and to begin at once to mobilize support against the Democratic National Committee controlled by Smith adherents.

Analysis of the mechanics by which he had carried New York State while Al lost it confirmed the wisdom of this approach. The Democratic candidates had run fairly evenly, with Smith slightly ahead in the city and Roosevelt slightly ahead outside it. Why, then, the difference in the outcome? The statistics gave the answer: more than a hundred thousand upstate Republicans who had voted for Hoover had refused to vote for their gubernatorial candidate, Albert Ottinger, who was a Jew. In Erie County, the defection had been open. Whether Roosevelt consciously recognized it or not, there was sufficient evidence of the importance of evading the religious issue. During the campaign he had spoken out vigorously against bigotry. But the result had demonstrated it was not wise to do so. His distant cousin, Nicholas Roosevelt, warned him of the danger. He would need Republican votes "if he ever was to be elected President." Almost at once, therefore, F.D.R. began to detach himself from Smith and from the issues with which Smith had been identified.

There was an immediate awkwardness in the change of administration. Al, as was the custom for outgoing governors, moved out of the Executive Mansion and into a suite at the Hotel DeWitt Clinton to make room for his successor. He offered also to be of any aid he could, while Roosevelt took hold of the reins. He had done the same in 1921 when control of the state had passed to the Republican Nathan Miller.

To the new governor this step seemed designed to con

tinue Smith's control of the state while he himself was made a figurehead. Quickly he rebuffed Smith's advance; and thereafter he almost never consulted his predecessor on matters of policy. When Smith asked for an advance copy of the new governor's first message to the Legislature, Roosevelt agreed to send it and then forgot to do so. Significantly, that address was brief, was devoted largely to rural problems, and made hardly a reference to what had gone before.

At the same time, Roosevelt had begun to oust the Smith officeholders and to use the patronage to build a following of his own. He refused to reappoint Robert Moses, thereby settling a personal score with the Secretary of State who had once declined to put Roosevelt's personal secretary on the state payroll. The new governor also failed to find a place in his administration for Belle Moskowitz, although Smith asked him to do so. His appointments were to build up his own strength; so, for instance, Moses's job went to Ed Flynn, politically powerful boss of the Bronx. Meanwhile, James A. Farley and Louis Howe set to work to recruit support throughout the country.

Smith was hurt. Still underrating Roosevelt's ability and not impressed with his presidential ambitions, Al thought these were the foolish gestures of an inexperienced man, capriciously destroying an organization it had taken years to build. There was pain also in the form of it. Roosevelt was never at his best in getting rid of people no longer useful to him. The lack of directness and candor in his actions left a bitter impression of shiftiness, of disloyalty, and of ingratitude.

Not that Smith for the moment had any intention of

involving himself in state affairs. His offer of aid had been a gesture of solicitude for the success of the new administration. He himself was to be fully occupied with other matters in 1929 and 1930.

Immediately after the election, Smith had announced, "As far as running for office again is concerned — that's finished." He meant it at the moment. He was fifty-five years old and terribly disappointed. He had gotten about as far as he could in politics; there was still time to try his hand at something else. And even if he should at some later date change his mind, it was strategically sound to withdraw at the moment.

There was an indication of his new attitude in April 1929, when Olvany resigned as head of Tammany Hall. Smith was one of the elders chosen to designate a new leader. He refused to act, although power then descended by default to Jimmy Walker, who put in John F. Curry, no friend of Al's.

Smith by no means intended to lose touch with what was going on. He was concerned with the future of his associates and resolved to continue the fight for the principles in which he believed. "I will never lose my interest in public affairs, that is a sure thing," he proclaimed. Significantly, when a group of liberal Democrats formed the Jeffersonian Society in May 1929, they dedicated it to "the principles of Alfred E. Smith."

As in 1920 when he had left public office, so in 1928, it seemed logical to turn to another area in which a good man could succeed, business. In the excited atmosphere of the boom, his friends were multiplying their fortunes — making good in a big way. He too could apply his administrative talents to enterprises that might add to his fame and his wealth. Being governor had not been financially remunerative.

Smith had never been hostile to capitalism as such, only to its abuses. He had always recognized the possibility of achievement in business. If the biggest prize in politics was out of reach, perhaps he could make his mark in this other way.

These thoughts ran through his mind as he agreed to take part in a grandiose enterprise that developed after the election. The project had for some time been shaping up within a circle of Raskob's New York associates. They had taken over the site of the old Waldorf-Astoria Hotel and were now resolved to build upon it the largest and highest edifice in the world — a monument to the constructive ability of New York. The name itself, the Empire State Building, was symbolic. Smith became its president and thereafter was heavily involved in its affairs.

In the heady atmosphere of 1928 and 1929, however, businessmen did not confine themselves to one task; successful enterprise proliferated. Everyone was on the alert for opportunities to spread out, to buy into dealerships, to take a flyer in real estate, to promote a fight or a play, to invest in new ideas. Many a man was building a pyramid of diversified holdings up which he would climb to the top.

At the pinnacle was the banker. It was a fine thing of course to sit in a polished office and to control the flow of cash across the mahogany. All the chances in the world passed across the desk for a man to be in on. Anyone who looked back at the last forty years could see that the financiers had dominated the economic order. And every ambitious man whose fortune grew large enough dreamed of taking a hand in banking.

It went without saying that the old, well-established institutions were not eager to make places on their boards for newcomers, particularly for such as were not graced by good family, proper education, or membership in the right clubs. That was not, however, an insuperable obstacle so long as it was possible to create new banks. Precisely because they were somewhat restricted, the opportunities in finance were particularly attractive to people who had risen fast and who hoped thus to acquire status as well as power. So, Jewish clothing manufacturers formed the Bank of the United States; Francesco M. Ferrari and his Italian associates set up the City Trust Company; and James J. Riordan, Al's friend, gathered together a group of contractors and other Irish-Americans in the County Trust Company. Al became a director of the institution.

These were more than businesses. Such enterprises gave visible form to the desire of new groups for recognition and status. Men who had themselves come up the hard way aspired thus to set themselves and their children up in life, and not merely as manufacturers and contractors still linked to the sewing machine and the shovel, but as bankers. American society in the early part of 1929 offered no better way up.

Toward the end of the year, it all changed. The effect of the stock-market crash on men of this sort was crushing. The newly reared structures of their fortunes were rarely able to weather the storm. Unlike the older families whose holdings were buttressed by gilt-edged securities, these lacked the roots to hold them up through the crisis; and the older banking and industrial firms were not altogether reluctant to see the upstarts go under. The failure of the City Trust Company earlier in the year had been taken quite placidly; Governor Roosevelt did little about the warning of Robert Moses that its fall revealed a situation that would threaten other institutions as well. Nor, later, would the bankers stir to save the Bank of the United States.

The crash, in time, affected men of every rank in every part of the nation. But there was a special poignancy in the impact upon those newer Americans who thought they had arrived in 1929. For many an Irishman and Italian and Jew, the collapse swept away wealth and station and also the beautiful dream of a golden land that was every man's opportunity. Al himself suffered. This was a second defeat, as calamitous in its results as that in politics a year earlier.

The foundations of the Empire State Building had already been laid when the crisis came. It was too late to draw back or to halt the enterprise, even had pride permitted it. Yet it became increasingly difficult to find the means for carrying on the project; the great steel structure rose higher and higher month after month to be completed in record time; but it could not outdistance the steadily lengthening shadows of eventual failure. The mood of 1930 was no longer one to encourage promoters in a belief in the building's full occupancy. Al found the job almost full-time, as his energies were absorbed in the problems of construction and finance.

Distractions of another kind also worried him. On Friday, November 8, 1929, James Riordan, his intimate friend and business associate, committed suicide. Smith wept in the shock of the personal loss, dismayed that a good Catholic should thus be driven to a step the penalty of which was eternal perdition. It must have been that his problems had driven him insane; and a fine man he had been, lovable and a good companion.

Coming when it did, Riordan's death inevitably produced fears for the financial stability of the County Trust Company. To prevent a run, the news was withheld until after the bank had closed for the week end; and further to restore public confidence Raskob became its president and Smith the chairman of the Board. Other friends moved in to back up the bank and, with their aid, it came shakily through the crisis. But it was another drain on Smith's time. This was altogether apart from the fact that the dead man had let several members of Al's family in on some hot tips. Without telling Smith, they had speculated in the market, were wiped out, and now needed assistance.

Riordan's death uncovered yet another problem that would bring Al many a heartache. The campaign of 1928 had been expensive; and the big-money men of the Democratic Party had not been lavish in their donations, partly out of lack of enthusiasm for a liberal candidate and partly out of the foreknowledge of defeat. The most substantial gifts, with few exceptions, had come from Smith's own group.

As the campaign proceeded, the pressure for funds grew more intense. Raskob had planned to spend four million, but out of his own political inexperience and enthusiasm had let the total climb up toward five. You had to have a heart and it would be a shame for all that to let the want of a few dollars ruin their man's chance. Riordan, out of the love of Smith, determined not to allow financial limitations to stand in the way. The County Trust would help, and after Al won there would be plenty of men anxious to make up the deficit.

Riordan resolved to allow the County Trust to lend a million dollars to the Democratic National Committee. Since the law prohibited corporations from making political contributions, it was necessary that some of Smith's friends endorse the note. That was all a mere formality, of course. Riordan assured the signers that they would never have to pay. They were almost all Irish, all eager to believe victory was possible in 1928; and they gave no thought to what might happen in defeat. This was an act of friendship, of which Al himself knew nothing.

Now it was all in the open. It was painful enough to know that the man had thus sacrificed himself; and to know also that so many other good friends had been troubled. It was more painful still, as officer of the bank, to be forced to take steps to collect. Some of the signers, notably Mara, proved recalcitrant, and that ultimately led to a long lawsuit which the County Trust won, but in which no one was the victor. Meanwhile Mara, who was in financial straits, was bringing suit against Gene Tunney; and into that case too Al's name was tangentially drawn. The promoters had once thought of asking the Governor to persuade the Boxing Commission to allow Tunney rather than Wills to fight Dempsey for the championship. There was nothing to it; the Governor had never been approached, and the fight had been held in Philadelphia. But it was all a mess.

In these difficult days of 1929 and 1930, Smith had little enough time for politics. In business, too, the big prize had slipped away; it took all he had to hold on. "Poor Al," he knew his friends were saying.

Yet he was determined to fight back; and his interest in public affairs was strong as ever. In 1929, he had gone

to dinner with a group of Harvard professors. Awkward
and uneasy when he was asked to follow the philosopher
Alfred North Whitehead as speaker, he launched finally
into a talk on state government that held his audience
spellbound. It was good to know that the old touch was
still there. A little later, at a dinner with Bernard Baruch,
he discovered that the other guest, Winston Churchill, had
asked specifically to meet him; and they went off to Tammany Hall together for a gay evening. There were still
those who valued the old man.

Politics took a new turn in 1930 when the fall elections
brought the Democrats back. The depression had effected
a violent shift in voters' allegiance and had given new
value to the presidential nomination in 1932. The party
took control of many state administrations; and by the
time the seventy-second Congress met, it had acquired a
majority in the House of Representatives. With the aid
of the insurgent Republicans, it could also have its way in
the Senate.

To capitalize upon the opportunity, however, it had to
define its stand as a party. Traditionally it did so only once
every four years, in the platform written by the convention; and usually that chow mein of platitudes was con-
veniently forgotten after November. Between elections,
policy, in so far as it was fixed at all, was established in
Congress with each faction going its own way. "The truth
is," the Baltimore *Sun* observed in 1929, "the Democratic
Party doesn't exist between elections."

Smith had no elaborate theories about party or Congressional responsibility. But he knew who was who in the
national Legislature; an anachronistic committee system

and the lack of opposition in the South gave control in the capital to the very men who had deserted him in 1928. There was only one alternative: to induce the National Committee, the one permanent body representative of the whole party, to speak out on the important issues, as the New York State Committee had since 1923. Joe Tumulty and other influential Democrats had advocated such a course since November 1928.

On the problems raised by the depression, there seemed few significant differences of opinion in Congress or among the prospective candidates. But Prohibition was as thorny a question as ever; for the line between Wet and Dry was identical with that between the tolerant and the bigoted, between the city and the country. Since 1928 the Drys had been busy in the effort to consolidate their gains. Immediately after the election Bishop Cannon had called for the ouster of Raskob and for a purge of the committee; and there had been no abatement thereafter in the flow of their propaganda.

Smith and his friends on the committee, Raskob and Jouett Shouse, were equally determined to bring the issue out into the open. When the committee met in March 1931, they asked it to take a clear stand in favor of the repeal of the Prohibition Amendment. No doubt they expected that Cordell Hull of Tennessee and Cameron Morrison of North Carolina would oppose them and that Joe Robinson of Arkansas would plead for party harmony. But it came as a surprise and shock to learn, shortly before the meeting, that Roosevelt and Farley had entered into an alliance with the Southerners to defeat the proposal.

That alliance made sense to Roosevelt. The tactical victory made it unnecessary for him to take a stand with either the Wets or the Drys; and it earned him the support of the Southerners who, as Hull said, turned to him "as the most effective way of killing off Smith." In return, however, he had been forced to agree that "between Conventions, the spokesmen on policy matters are, primarily, the Democratic members of the Senate and House." It would take six years and the failure of the purge of 1938 before he learned the price he had paid — the permanent surrender to a bloc of Southern senators of an effective veto over national legislation.

For Smith, the setback added to the evidence of Roosevelt's unreliability. Two years earlier, in January 1929, the two men had tried briefly to talk about mending political fences and had been forced to move to the safe ground of a discussion of the state budget. Already then Al had found his successor unwilling to confront the issues he himself considered important. In March 1931, that impression was decisively confirmed. Knowing of Roosevelt's negotiations with Hull, Byrd, and the other Southerners, Smith refused to listen over the telephone to the usual plausible evasions.

Even then, Al had not made up his mind to be again a candidate, although the nomination was certainly more valuable than it had been after the 1928 election when he had announced he would not again seek the Presidency. Probably the thought crossed his mind that he deserved another chance, but far more important was the insistence that the candidate, whoever he be, vindicate his own position and prove that the hatreds and prejudices of 1928 had been an aberration.

That consideration dominated Smith's actions through the next year. A variety of hopefuls were in the field —

Albert Ritchie of Maryland, Newton Baker of Ohio, and John Garner of Texas, as well as Roosevelt and Smith. Let them each pursue the quest; no one of them was likely to gain the necessary two-thirds and Roosevelt would be at a particular disadvantage without the support of his own state. That was also the attitude of Raskob and Shouse who wished the candidate — whoever he was — to be dependent upon their aid in the National Committee.

Smith was still not adamantly opposed to Roosevelt. Through 1931 and on into 1932 there was no effort to stop Farley's persistent raids into the Smith camp. Al made no objection when his close friend James Hoey or such influential Democrats as Ed Flynn and Herbert Lehman informed him that they would support Roosevelt. He only wondered why Roosevelt himself made no move to discuss the matter with him.

In December 1931 Clark Howell, publisher of the Atlanta *Constitution* and F.D.R.'s emissary, visited Smith. A long report of the conversation went back to Roosevelt, then in Warm Springs. Al pointed out that he was not unalterably opposed to Roosevelt. "Socially we are friends. He has always been kind to me and my family, and has gone out of his way to be agreeable to us." But he added, stamping his foot, "Do you know, by God, that he has never consulted me about a damn thing since he has been governor? He has taken bad advice and from sources not friendly to me. He has ignored me."

Smith made it clear that the resentment was more than personal. Millions of Northerners objected to the "way he had been treated" in 1928, and it was the obligation of every candidate to speak out on the subject of Prohibition. Roosevelt was dodging. "Why in hell don't he speak out?'

This "ain't the time for trimming." Al added that some of Roosevelt's "damn fool friends" were doing more harm than good and explicitly asked why the subject of the nomination had never been raised with him. "My recommendation," Howell concluded, "is that you see him upon your return to New York and talk with him on the subject. I think it will go a long way toward getting him in line. By handling him diplomatically I believe he will come around all right." A month later, Ed Flynn repeated the advice that the Governor see Smith.

Roosevelt could not do so. The latent uneasiness in his personal relationships with a man he admired but could not understand stood in the way. So did an unconscious and unrecognized sense of guilt. Back in February 1930 he had written in a jocular vein that it was high time for Smith to return to Albany. "Your granddaughter came to the house to spend the afternoon and five minutes after I had joined the party Mary was calling me 'Ganpa.' I felt highly honored and have certainly cut you out." A sensitive man could not altogether escape the moments of doubt as to whether he had not unfairly cut Al out in a wider sense.

It was not in Roosevelt's temperament to confront such a situation squarely. Then and later, for all his charm, he was awkward in the inability to look those to whom he could not be graciously acquiescent directly in the eye. He lacked the capacity for the straightforward no; and, in the unwillingness to deny a favor, to order a dismissal, to deliver bad news, slipped into the greater cruelty of deception. He could not look Smith in the face and say, It ought to be me, not you.

Most important of all, Roosevelt feared that an encounter with Smith would raise questions he did not wish to answer. As a candidate whose chief support came from outside his own state, he could not present himself to the convention merely as a favorite son. He had to hold the allegiance of scattered supporters in many parts of the country; and he could only do so by remaining vague on issues on which they differed. Yet through the latter half of 1931, Roosevelt had been under continual pressure to declare himself. Thus the insistent goading of William Randolph Hearst had finally compelled him to retreat from internationalism and to come out against American adherence to the League of Nations. From the frequent demands for a stand on Prohibition he took refuge in a moderate Wet-Dry equivocation calculated to antagonize no one. Roosevelt writhed at the thought of framing a reply should Smith ask him how he really stood on the Eighteenth Amendment and on the wider issues of which it was the symbol. Roosevelt preferred not to have Smith request him to antagonize the rural Protestant elements of the party whose support he thought was essential to his nomination and election.

As the election year opened and Smith's resentment mounted, Roosevelt continued to keep his distance. Word got back of rumors spread in the South and the West that Du Pont, Raskob and Smith were the agents of a Wall Street plot to stop Roosevelt. Al's sense of hurt rose also with reiteration of the argument that no Catholic could be elected in 1932. He was annoyed particularly when Arthur Mullen, typical of the timid Midwestern Catholics, told him outright, "We are tired of this religious issue." Maybe it was true, Smith thought, but was it necessary spinelessly to give in? For his part, the fight was worth continuing; and if he were himself not the victor, he would at least gather enough strength to make sure the candidate took a stand. His personal affairs were still a distraction with the County Trust and the Mancuso cases coming to trial. But he was resolute in making a test of his candidacy.

He found some encouragement in the New York State election of 1931. The Legislature, with Roosevelt's support, had submitted a reforestation amendment to the people. The proposal had the approval of Tammany and the rest of the Democratic Party, of the Republicans, of the conservationists and of the lumber interests. But it embodied a principle that Smith had fought since his own governorship; for it inserted into the Constitution a provision that belonged in the statute books and it made a paper commitment for a long time ahead that no future Legislature could be compelled to honor. Al came out against it.

The amendment carried by some 750,000 votes against 550,000. Some observers regarded this as a defeat for Smith. But he knew better. Not only did the objectionable program collapse within two years; but there was a more immediate cause of satisfaction. Most of the favorable votes had come from Republicans; the negative ones were preponderantly Democratic. The outcome showed how large a body of people he could sway by his mere say-so, without party or organization. He was determined to use this influence in the selection of a proper candidate.

The first six months of 1932 were consumed in oratory and the quest of delegates. It was clear, as Al put it, that what the country needed was another ex-President. He, Roosevelt, Ritchie, and the other prospective nominees now took to the platform to make known their availability for the task of easing Hoover into that status. On economic matters, there were then few fundamental divisions among Democratic candidates; the differences were more of style and personality.

In two January speeches, Smith set forth his view of the campaign issues in eloquent, forceful terms. Asking the party to make "a clean-cut, straightforward declaration, not only of principle, but of what we intend to do," he called for the immediate repeal of the Eighteenth Amendment and outlined an economic program. He pleaded for economy, efficiency and tariff reform. But more was needed in the "state of war" created by the depression. The federal government must assume the burden of relief the states could no longer bear; and a vast program of public works to create employment must be financed by borrowing, if necessary. He would "cut, slash, dig into, and run through all the red tape, and through all the statutory restrictions that are placed upon the government." If, he pointed out, "it is all right to put the credit of the government behind business, let the credit of the government be used to keep the wolf of hunger away from the doormat of millions of people." Early in February, he threw his hat into the ring. He would run if the convention chose him, although he would not make an active campaign for delegates.

These aggressive steps worried Roosevelt. When the implications of the reforestation vote sank in he spent a sleepless night and "never closed my eyes." His own January speeches had been mild. Still hedging on Prohibition in the wet city of Buffalo, he had weakened even further his weak statement of 1930. At a victory dinner in New York he had asked for tax reform and urged aid alike for big and little business, "without preferring one over the other." That speech had been well enough received; "but the major ovation of the evening was accorded former Governor Smith, although he was not present to hear it."

Smith's open candidacy dismayed the leaders of the Southern and Western wings of the party; they dreaded the "revival of the prohibition and religious issues" of 1928. Rumors spread that his successor had discovered he had been a "rotten" governor, that he was "an envious man who did not want one of his oldest friends to have that which he could not have himself." Most important of all, new emphasis was given to the accusation that he was just a tool of Wall Street conservatives to stop the liberal Roosevelt.

Roosevelt attempted to capitalize on that sentiment in a radio address in March. This speech opened dramatically. Using the same figure of speech as Smith, the state of war, he attacked the Hoover administration for seeking recovery through aid at the top of the economic pyramid, while neglecting the "forgotten men" who were its base. Roosevelt also ridiculed the notion that public works could solve the problems of unemployment. True recovery, he insisted, could only come through aid to the mass of the "forgotten men."

After the rhetorical flourishes of the opening paragraphs, the positive proposals that followed were innocuous enough — "fur overcoats for elephants," the boys would have said — aid to agriculture, assistance to small bankers and homeowners, and adjustments in the tariff. These suggestions revealed that Roosevelt had in mind the same "forgotten man" as William Graham Sumner, from whom Raymond Moley had borrowed the term. Roosevelt made it clear a few weeks later that he referred to the millions who were "not employees in the strict sense of the word — the farmers, the small business man, the professional people."

If Smith had been at all undecided, this speech confirmed his opposition to Roosevelt. On Jefferson Day, April 14, Al delivered his answer. After discussing the relationship of international trade to foreign debts and the tariff, he reaffirmed his faith in the public works program. He repudiated the slur by a "prominent Democrat" that this was only a "stop gap"; "who ever said that it was anything else?" That made it none the less essential to succor the industrial laborers to whose plight Roosevelt had paid no attention.

The statement about the forgotten men had been sheer demagoguery. It touched off memories of the vague Bryanite oratory Al had always distrusted. The small-town bankers and the farmers were not more forgotten, more worthy of aid, than the industrial laborers. Their votes were more strategically disposed, that was all. Roosevelt had injected a false and dangerous doctrine into the campaign. Recovery was not to be attained either at the top or at the bottom, but all along the line of an interdependent economic system. By setting class against class in his own interest, Roosevelt had joined Huey Long and Father Coughlin and the wild-eyed agrarians who used group hatred and the delusion that they could share the wealth as the cloaks for their own ambition.

Faith in America meant something else to Smith. Genuinely offended by the "endeavor to delude the poor people of this country to their ruin," he announced: "I will take off my coat and fight to the end against any candidate who persists in any demagogic appeal to the masses of the working people of this country to destroy themselves by setting class against class and rich against poor." He warned that "the disposition to gloss over controversial questions in an attempt to please both sides" would bring forth a meaningless platform and a colorless candidate. "Only by courage, by foresight and by careful preparation of the platform without compromise" could the country win. And if the whole country did not gain by the election, "what difference does it make which party wins?"

The exchange continued on into May. But the two men were no longer listening to each other; and in any case, they had lost the capacity to understand each other's language. Smith heard only the vague, evasive generalities of his opponent's pronouncements and missed the overtones of a conception that gradually took form in Roosevelt's entourage, that of a positive role for the state in the national economy. And Roosevelt, blinded by anxiety and perhaps by guilt, persuaded himself that Al's specific concrete proposals concealed pitfalls by which the conservatives hoped to entrap him. The lines were drawn.

A variety of factors had pushed Smith to a decision. Perhaps his own ambition would have led him there in any case; once there was a likelihood of a Democratic victory he certainly felt he deserved another chance. Then too, his wife and some of his friends were eager still to see him in the White House. But more important was the development of an identification between Roosevelt and the forces that had won in 1928. Smith could not, in self-respect, or with any regard to the principles for which he stood, easily acquiesce.

As the alignment of forces proceeded, Smith saw that the struggle involved not him alone but the fate of many others. The Roosevelt people had marshaled their strength where they could; their victory would bring into power, at the expense of Smith's allies, elements against which he had long fought.

In New York City, for instance, they had an arrangement with James J. Hines, an unscrupulous West Side district leader hostile to Smith, who would later spend a term in jail. At the same time, they were conducting a flirtation with Smith's enemies in Tammany Hall, and notably with John F. Curry. The Governor's solicitude for Mayor Walker, then under removal charges, seemed sinister. Smith, the idol of the East Side, had no fear that any Manhattan delegate would turn against him. But why was Roosevelt not being forthright?

In Massachusetts, where David I. Walsh and Joseph Ely, Smith's friends, had led the Democratic Party toward a constructive program for two decades, the Roosevelt people had struck up an alliance with James Michael Curley, the prototype of everything that Smith abominated. A politician who had already served the first of his richly deserved prison terms, Curley's stock in trade had been the appeal to the narrow clannishness of his group. Unlike Smith, he had consistently labored to widen rather than to bridge the differences between the Irish and their fellow citizens. In Massachusetts as elsewhere, a Roosevelt victory threatened to defeat those who had been leading the urban machines toward political maturity and to elevate the freebooters like Hines and Curley.

It was equally galling to see the traitors of 1928 advance to positions of intimacy with the Governor of New York.

Louis Howe was inviting Dan Roper of South Carolina to take a prominent, if surreptitious, part in the campaign; and throughout the South and West men who had sat on their hands four years earlier were preparing to take power behind the Roosevelt façade.

Al approached the convention in good spirits. He had the support of liberal columnists like Heywood Broun, of the Scripps-Howard chain, and of the metropolitan and Eastern press, which acclaimed him as the "one statesman who isn't afraid to speak his mind," and condemned his opponent as a "master of evasion." Roosevelt had the approval of the Western and Southern newspapers, but often, as the Norfolk *Virginian-Pilot* put it, out of repugnance "for another perilous war with religious bigotry."

Furthermore, in three critical primaries, the Roosevelt bandwagon seemed to have been stopped. In Massachusetts, where the issue was most clearly drawn, Smith led by a three-to-one majority. In Pennsylvania and in California he had made an excellent showing. These tests, Walter Lippmann explained, disposed completely of Roosevelt's claim that he was "the idol of the masses, opposed only by the international bankers, the power trust, and Mr. Raskob." The urban laborers of the East had detected "something hollow in him, something synthetic, something pretended and calculated." Whatever his following in the rural West and South, he had little strength in the industrial East and Midwest. The Roosevelt states on the map might cover a lot of ground, but as one of Al's supporters noted, "It's votes not acres that count."

The Smith forces entered the convention that met in Chicago on June 27 with less than half as many delegates as Roosevelt. But Roosevelt's followers were almost all from south of the Mason-Dixon line and west of the Mississippi. If the initial Roosevelt drive could be stopped, the two-thirds rule would bring it to a halt. And even if Smith should not ultimately be chosen, the standard-bearer would be someone acceptable to him.

Smith, however, was to be decisively defeated. In the last analysis, Roosevelt proved the abler politician — less scrupulous, more free to maneuver, and hampered by fewer enmities.

The opening skirmishes favored Al. Smith's friends on the National Committee arranged the distribution of spectator tickets so that he woud have a favorable gallery. The Roosevelt forces were defeated in the effort to overturn the two-thirds rule. More important, the platform was largely drafted by the Smith men on the resolutions committee. Despite the opposition of Cordell Hull and the Roosevelt camp, the majority plank calling for outright repeal was adopted. Smith, speaking for the majority, reminded the party that Hoover attempted to carry water on both shoulders; when his investigating committee brought in a Wet report, "he sent for the blotting paper and dried it up." Al's plea for candor touched off a tumultuous ovation that brought a lump to his throat "as wave after wave of cheers swept through the stadium." It was something when a delegate from Texas spoke up against those who had "crucified him on a cross of religious intolerance" in 1928.

But in a more serious test over the choice of a permanent chairman, Al went down to defeat and that presaged the final outcome. The Smith group had agreed to accept Alben Barkley as temporary chairman if the Roosevelt forces would take Shouse as permanent presiding officer.

Naïvely relying upon their faith that a deal was a deal, they were surprised to discover that the Roosevelt men advanced Senator Thomas J. Walsh for the post. When Walsh was carried into the office by a hundred-vote majority, it was clear that Roosevelt could only be stopped by a prolonged stalemate.

Governor Joseph B. Ely put Smith in nomination with an eloquent but unwelcome speech that harked back to 1928. He could explain why Massachusetts had gone Democratic. "But no man has ever stated in public what caused our friends from the South to become Republican." Let the convention exorcise the ghosts of other years. Had not "the prejudices of our Protestant ancestors" long since "been wiped away by many a successful experience" in which men of whatever creed were safely entrusted with the reins of government? "The small voice of the inarticulate souls of" millions of Americans, begged "for the leadership of one of their own."

Off the floor, however, strenuous efforts were in progress to avoid a stalemate. On the first ballot, although Roosevelt led with 661 votes as against Smith's 201, a hundred more were needed for the necessary two-thirds majority. Given the disposition of the other favorite sons, the deficiency could be made up only from the Texas and California delegations pledged to Garner. The decision thus rested in the hands of McAdoo and Hearst, both old and bitter enemies of Al Smith. Almost at once, the lines were out for a deal to let the Garner votes go to Roosevelt in return for the Vice-Presidency. Roper and Curley were among those prominent in making the arrangement, an illustration of the wisdom of attaching them to the Roosevelt cause.

Again Smith was caught unawares, relying upon an understanding with McAdoo that neither would release his delegates without informing the other. Desperate efforts to reach Garner when the word got out proved unavailing. No one answered the telephone. On the fourth ballot, Roosevelt was nominated, with Smith and his allies bitter to the end. Garner received the Vice-Presidency as a matter of course. The West and the South had won no greater victory since 1912.

Few at the convention understood its meaning as well as Ed Flynn, who had labored hard for Roosevelt. Early in the proceedings, Smith had reproached the Bronx leader, "Ed, you are not representing the people of Bronx County in your support of Roosevelt. You know the people of Bronx County want you to support me." Flynn had stayed with Franklin Roosevelt; a promise was a promise. But the nagging rebuke lingered in his mind, as McAdoo — the old foe and now friend — rose to transfer California's vote to Roosevelt. And when the Presidency was settled, Ed thought, Well, for the Vice-Presidency it ought to be someone other than Garner, someone less distasteful to the Northeast Catholics. A Westerner, even, would be better than "a representative of perhaps, bigotry's banner state," as the *Catholic Mirror* described the Texan.

Flynn got nowhere, however, in the effort to convince the Roosevelt leaders. It was not alone the obligation to Garner that was decisive, but the larger consideration that above all else reconstitution of the Solid South was preeminently important.

V I I I

A World Unknown

THERE WERE SOME in the cheering crowd in Chicago who rejoiced not only because Roosevelt had won, but also because Smith had been routed.

The Roosevelt leaders, however, could not afford to gloat over Smith's defeat. With the nomination secure, the whole focus of their strategy shifted. The vote of the West and the South was still important. But it was by no means as critical in the election as it had been in the convention. The November decision was more likely to be shaped in the populous states of Pennsylvania, New Jersey, New York, and Massachusetts, where Smith had only recently proven his popularity. It was essential that he be appeased and take his stand on Roosevelt's side.

That summer the outcome of the election seemed by no means certain. Some of Roosevelt's advisers in Albany, uneasy when they heard that Al was on his way home, hastened to placate him. He had failed to make the nomination unanimous and had refused to stay to greet the victor; and without his active aid, there was no telling what would happen in the Northeast. Mrs. Roosevelt was

instructed to send Bernard Shientag to meet Smith's train
at Harmon and to learn his intentions; and soothing over-
tures toward a reconciliation followed.

Smith let them wait. He knew that ultimately he would
come out for Roosevelt. On the way back from Chicago
he had discussed the whole matter with Judge Proskauer.
Al was mad — mad at having lost and at the manner of the
defeat. Nevertheless, party loyalty and the necessity of
taking defeat like a good sport left him no alternative.
Furthermore, although he was skeptical that Roosevelt
would long adhere to it, the platform adopted at Chicago
was precisely such a clear statement of policy as Smith had
demanded. To the extent that the election was a test of
issues as well as of men, Al knew he would speak out for
the party ticket. But he would do so independently and in
his own good time.

The proper moment came at the selection of the slate
for state offices. Roosevelt and Smith supported the candidacy of Herbert Lehman for the governorship; Curry
wanted the place for one more responsive to Tammany
influence. Al intervened. He had helped draw Lehman
into politics, had induced him to run for the lieutenant-
governorship in 1928, and had benefited from his contribution of five hundred thousand dollars to the Democratic
campaign fund. Furthermore Lehman had demonstrated
the ability to handle the office successfully.

Smith laid it on the line to Curry. If the Democrats
failed to nominate Lehman, Al would run for mayor the
next year and take control of the city away from Tammany.

"On what ticket?" sneered the boss.

"On a Chinese laundry ticket, I can beat you and your
crowd" was the answer; and Curry yielded. Appropriately

enough Roosevelt and Smith exchanged greetings and seemed to have effected a reconciliation at the state convention which finally nominated Lehman.

Smith campaigned independently in the Eastern urban centers where it did Roosevelt the most good. Everywhere he was warmly welcomed. He followed his own line, attacking Hoover's stand on Prohibition and criticizing his slowness in making effective any public works or relief programs. "In the picture of the twenty-mule team pulling the borax wagon," Al pointed out, "if all the mules do not pull" the wagon does not budge. In the Republican administration, "nineteen of the mules are lying on the ground asleep and the twentieth is giving a halfhearted pull."

At the same time, he called for national unity. In a country in which individual initiative and the opportunity to rise were characteristic there was no room for class hatred or for the "Communist, the Fascist, or the Junker" who thrived on it. At Newark he made a final attack upon racial and religious bigotry. To the dismay of those Roosevelt managers who hoped to forget 1928, Al reminded his audience of what the Republicans had said, and the Methodists, and Mabel Walker Willebrandt.

But his tone softened as the prospects of party victory brightened. "There can be no bigotry and there can be no resentment in the Catholic heart," he pointed out in his talk at Boston. "It cannot be there." Only he insisted on affirming what he had been taught "in our elementary schools," that "Almighty God himself made this country . . . to . . . be open to the world as a haven of refuge and a place of repose for the poor and oppressed of every land."

Smith was pleased at the outcome of the balloting. The landslide that swept Roosevelt into office was even greater than .hat of 1928. Only six states remained loyal to the Republicans; and their popular vote of 15,700,000 was far outdistanced by the Democratic total of 22,800,000. The magnitude of the victory no doubt gave Al reason to believe that any opponent could have beaten Hoover. But if ever the thought crossed his mind that for him, too, the nomination might this time have meant the election, he never gave it expression. He was determined to co-operate.

During the interlude between the election and the inauguration there were occasional speculations in the press that Smith might assume some important post in the new administration. As late as May 1933, he told his daughter that he was eager to serve in the national emergency.

But it was not to be so. Place after place was filled in the old departments and in the new agencies. But no offer was made to him. Whether he would actually have accepted it or not, it was galling not to be asked, particularly since there seemed to be room for unfriendly Southerners and even for Republicans. For that matter other respectable people of good judgment valued his services more; in the last month of 1932 he had been a member of the National Transportation Commission that investigated the plight of the railroads.

Smith retained an interest in public service; there had been a wistful note in his suggestion a year earlier that the runner-up in a presidential election should be made a member-at-large of the Senate; and he later commented to Winston Churchill on the "lack of continuity in American public life for party leaders." He continued to work for certain projects initiated under his governorship. He thus testified skillfully before the Seabury Committee on municipal reform, went down to plead with the R.F.C. for a loan for Jones Beach. A long cross-examination that finally satisfied the directors put him in good humor. At the end, he requested and received permission to ask one question, in return, "Where do we go to get the check?"

All that seemed over, however, as the months went by. No doubt there now came back the sentences from a speech of Bourke Cockran's that he had once memorized: "Is the politician happy? Far from it. When the scepter of power finally drops from his nerveless fingers, he is condemned to an isolation the more unbearable because of the adulation to which he has become accustomed."

The exclusion from any responsibility for action crippled Smith as a politician. He had never been a theoretician, but had always formed his opinions through contact with concrete problems. Now condemned to be a bystander and a detached critic, he would ever after rest his judgments on the experience of an earlier, bygone era. His ideas would become rigid, unresponsive to new situations.

Furthermore, he lost the audience that had theretofore been an essential element of his strength. For a time, he dealt with public questions in the columns of the *New Outlook*. But the written word did not come easily to him, although some of his friends helped him at the task. The pages of a magazine did not offer the same opportunity as the platform for gauging the responsiveness of listeners, for getting across through an identification with their moods and interests.

From 1933 onward, therefore, the man lost his grip. His personal difficulties were more troubling than ever. He was involved in a fight over control of the Meenan Coal

Company. His son, Alfred, who finally terminated an unhappy marriage by a separation, became entangled with
blackmailers and could hardly keep his head above water.
Meanwhile, the Empire State Building — that symbol of
all the lost hopes of 1928 — proved unprofitable beyond
the most pessimistic predictions.

The old friends began to drop away. Some, like Frances
Perkins, were drawn into the orbit of the New Deal. Belle
Moskowitz died. Robert Moses, a Republican, ran for
governor in 1934 against Lehman; and Smith satisfied
neither candidate by his moderate support of the Democrat.

More and more Al became dependent upon his immediate family and a hard core of friends, mostly Irish,
who remained tied to him in interest and outlook. Some
of them, like Kenny and Raskob, were still wealthy; others
had suffered in the depression and struggled to keep their
standard of living from slipping downward. They, and
Smith along with them, longed for a restoration of the
good old days when ability and ingenuity could earn an
enterprising man an immense fortune. Inevitably their
attitudes influenced him; their situation and his own made
him resentful of rising income and inheritance taxes. He
himself found it a struggle to keep the apartment at 51
Fifth Avenue going.

Yet in the first year of the new administration his attitude was flexible. He led the New York delegation that
marched proudly at the inauguration; he called upon the
President to exercise war powers in the emergency. He
was willing to give the NRA a trial in the hope it would
improve labor conditions. In the fall of 1933 there was
talk of a Smith-Roosevelt alliance to oust Curry and to

take over control of New York City; and in the spring of 1934 he broke with the *New Outlook,* in part because of its harsh criticism of the President. In the first year of the new administration, Al approved of some aspects of the New Deal and disapproved of others, sometimes as too conservative, sometimes as too radical.

At the start, Smith was critical of Roosevelt, yet tolerant. Like most Democrats in November and December, 1932, he felt the need for efficiency and economy in government, for relief from excessive taxation, and for tariff reform. He expected repeal of the Eighteenth Amendment and an expanded public works program. In the spring of 1933, the new administration seemed to take the right turn, providing "prompt and constructive leadership," guiding "public opinion wisely, and restoring morale and confidence." Smith praised the President for acting in the banking crisis, for helping to repeal the Eighteenth Amendment, for regulating the sale of securities and for recognizing the Soviet Union.

But Al also was watchful for signs of failure. The administration seemed too slow in dealing with the needs of the industrial population. More vigor was essential in the reform of labor law, in the provision for unemployment insurance and in the regulation of wages and hours. The President did nothing to admit the refugees from Hitlerism or to review immigration laws based on "fantastic Aryan theories rather than American principles." In the matter of housing, Al wished Roosevelt to avoid the mistakes of Hoover, who "promised relief and gave nothing but three cheers." Loans to homeowners ought to be more liberal and an entirely new policy was required to aid the lower income groups. Schemes for limited dividend corporations had failed; now the task would have to be undertaken through municipal housing authorities assisted by federal subsidies and local tax exemption. If that did not work, then slum clearance should be "a straight government enterprise." Smith cautioned the real estate interests against "stupid or selfish obstruction" and warned the administration against neglect of its responsibilities.

Part of the New Deal's trouble came from inefficiency. In October, 1933, Al pointed out that administrative reorganization was essential to speed up the work of the PWA. The prodigal carelessness of the inexperienced men at the helm in Washington offended one whose whole career had emphasized efficiency. Besides, the job was not getting done, projects were not taking form quickly enough. Yet there was no reform. Instead, "one of the absent-minded professors had played anagrams with the alphabet soup" and the CWA, a new agency, arose to stand beside the old one. This disorder was unfortunately free of criticism from those in the know. No local official "who has hung up an empty stocking over the municipal fireplace is going to shoot Santa Claus just before a hard Christmas."

Mingled among these sober and responsible comments was criticism of quite another sort. Smith still displayed an obsessive concern with the lesson of Prohibition. The Eighteenth Amendment was gone; but he, who had suffered so much in fighting it, saw analogous threats in a number of unexpected places. Under the pretext of legislating morality, there was a danger of government interference with individual rights in the federal child labor amendment, in Tugwell's proposals to amend the pure food and drug act, and in the NRA.

His deepest fears, however, were aroused when he detected in the government's gold policy signs of the agrarianism he detested. He had no objection to inflation as such, if only it were controlled; and he stood by the last party platform which had called for "a sound currency to be preserved at all hazards, and an international monetary conference" to "consider the rehabilitation of silver and related questions." Back in March he had warned Roosevelt to get rid "of the counsels of the minority of bigots, fanatics, populists, demagogues, mountebanks, and crackpots" — the fanatics "who dragged religion and liquor into politics; the populists who blighted the party" with "free silver and other economic heresies"; the demagogues "without loyalty to person or principle"; and "the mountebanks with their clownish antics and irresponsible raving against millionaires and big business." These had all become one compound threat to American institutions; and Roosevelt was not to be allowed to yield to them. Toward the end of the year, as the government seemed to take a Bryanite course approved by Huey Long and Father Coughlin, Smith's hostility grew. He attacked the "baloney dollar." In return he was accused by the radio priest of having sold out to J. P. Morgan back in 1927; and Hearst from San Simeon announced, "Mr. Roosevelt is striving to get the country away from the blood money of the Shylocks" against the "international bankers who have robbed us and betrayed us in the past and are apparently striving to establish the dollar of depression so they can plunder us again."

The reaction of the New Dealers intensified Smith's alienation. This was a crusade with all the zeal, enthusiasm and dedication of a marching army. Men convinced they were on their way to rescue the country from disaster and to redeem for it a new promised land were not likely to be tolerant of those who fell out of step. There was no room for carping criticism. Slackers who wasted time on debate were enemies, proclaimed Donald Richberg just before he left the ranks and was himself declared a traitor. Even to lunch with an outsider was to attract suspicion. Raymond Moley, Hugh Johnson, Herbert Lehman and others would before long suffer as deserters from the attacks of former colleagues.

Smith was the first to become a target. In February 1934 the President tried to use the PWA to undermine the position of Robert Moses, in a maneuver that Harold Ickes conceded was a "mistake from the start." Soon the old charges of a Wall Street conspiracy were revived, and Smith was vilified as a conservative anxious to make the rich richer. The rumor went around that the "big fellows" had put him on Fifth Avenue; that explained his opposition. Even his earlier record hadn't amounted to much; he had been just a party hack who had "never had an idea of his own," and who only made a pretense of liberalism for the sake of popularity or because advisers pushed him into it. Now he was angry because Roosevelt had not allowed him to run the state government in 1929.

As the word got back, Al's bitterness grew, and with it a rigid intransigence. Let them say what they would about Wall Street! "Unless you're ready to subscribe to the New Deal 100 per cent and sign your name on the dotted line you're a Tory, you're a prince of privilege, you're a reactionary, or you're an economic royalist." Well, Al thought, "No one who has gone through what I went through in 1928 is going to be worried by sneers and epithets." He offered no apology for being in business. "I didn't have a rich aunt or a rich uncle to take care of me." A sense of persecution dulled his critical faculties and brought him in 1934 to a position of complete enmity to the New Deal. Detached from the operations of government, he was unable thereafter to attain a balanced view of the political world around him. Nor did it help when one of the President's defenders implied that the United States needed its F.D.R. just as France had needed Danton and Russia Lenin.

Al failed, unfortunately, to understand the extent to which Roosevelt changed after 1934. To Smith, the President remained shallow, unreliable, tricky. Al was blind to the fact that the pressures of office were transforming the President as he himself had been transformed fifteen years earlier. Now it was F.D.R. who bore the burdens of decision and around whom the idea men moved in a whirl of sparkling stimuli.

Roosevelt had taken hold of the Presidency with some conception of objectives but without a clear notion of the methods by which to attain them. In the latter course of his campaign, between May 1932 and the election, as the brain trust took a larger part in shaping his speeches, he began to talk about the necessity for experimentation and for national planning. These ideas acquired an immediate relevance from the crisis into which the country had plunged by March 1933.

In the hectic first months of the new administration, ar exciting sense of new possibilities revived men's spirits. And Roosevelt learned by acting, as Smith was no longer able to. George Norris persuaded the President that Muscle Shoals contained the potential for a great regional plan;

and that became the basis for TVA. Fiorello LaGuardia
and Robert Wagner convinced him that an affirmation
of the rights to collective bargaining belonged in the National Industrial Recovery Act. The Wagner Act and
social security and wage and hour legislation showed a
concern for the urban workers that Smith should have
approved. Receptivity to new suggestions gave Roosevelt's
reactions a flexibility of the greatest importance in the face
of the changing problems of the times.

Neither Smith nor Roosevelt in 1932 understood how
radically Americans had been changing since 1928. Mass
unemployment, increasing misery, and the desperation
of men with no goal but survival had made a mockery
of risk. In the shocked awareness that the whole economy
could grind to a stop, that millions actually faced starva-
tion, only a collective effort to attain security made any
sense at all. The President's bouncy optimism, his willingness to try anything new, came to embody the hopes of
countless fearful Americans. As a result, there was a play-
back between him and them. It did not matter what he
had in mind originally; the industrial laborers, as well as
the farmers, identified themselves with the forgotten men
toward whom his solicitude extended. And the power of
their faith and dependence stretched the bounds of his
comprehension, so that in time his solicitude did extend
to them. For the moment, it was almost irrelevant that
Roosevelt said not a word about the old problems of the
Catholics and the other minorities. Other questions of security had more immediate importance.

Meanwhile Smith, who no longer had the stimulus of
an audience, continued to speak lines now grown stale.
Who listened as he worried about the plight of real estate,

about rising inheritance taxes, about the strangulation of new enterprises? Only a handful of embittered men, and they mostly industrialists equally foreign to the world developing around them.

The rigid core of this opposition in 1934 sought refuge from the persecutions of the New Deal in the Liberty League. Some members of this organization, like Smith himself and Shouse and Raskob, had had an honest title to the designation "liberal" in the 1920's. They had then fought for free speech, for states' rights, for individual freedom from government interference, and against bureaucracy and Prohibition. In the 1930's their attitudes had stiffened in a negative sterility. Other members, like James M. Beck, were old ideological foes of bureaucracy. And still others used the League as a shield for their own reactionary intentions. With the last-named Al was at first uncomfortable; in October 1934 he complained that the wrong people were too prominent in the organization. Alas, he had no other audience, and a deepening involvement brought him almost unwittingly into opposition against positions with which he had long been identified.

His critical comments, growing ever less temperate, reached their climax in January 1936, at the opening of another election year. At the League's annual dinner in the Mayflower in Washington, he spoke to a national radio hookup. He stood on the dais holding the prepared speech he was determined to give, although some of his friends had advised him against it. Looking down at the glittering ballroom, he realized he had no audience. What was he to the two thousand black ties and sequined gowns that waited in anticipation of the attack they had been told was coming?

He tried to envision the millions of homes into which his words would come. It took a straining of the imagination to try to picture what it was like out there. He could see only the microphone; and that "never nods approval. It never stimulates" by "expressing dissatisfaction with" a statement. It never warms with a handclap or shows appreciation at a sarcasm. "It is just a piece of cold metal suspended on a string, and it could not produce an original idea or an original thought in a century."

Steely hard words passed into the cold metal. Smith accused the New Deal of arraying class against class, of multiplying the bureaucracy, of having thrown the platform of 1932 "in the wastebasket." He asked the Democratic Party in the campaign that approached to renew its loyalty to the Constitution and to readopt the platform of 1932. So much was familiar.

Then an angry, unrestrained, tone crept into his voice as he explained why the New Deal had followed the course it did. "Here is the way it happened: The young brain trusters caught the Socialists in swimming and they ran away with their clothes." And he swung into an angry peroration that set Washington against Moscow, America against Communistic Russia, the Stars and Stripes against the Red Flag, and the Star-spangled Banner against the Internationale. No more than the metal were the people impressed.

In June, Smith joined a group of other conservative Democrats in the request for repudiation of the New Deal. He took a walk from the convention that renominated the President; and in October, in a bitter, sarcastic speech, he came out in support of Alf Landon. He had gone all the way.

About a week before the election, in Albany, he unconsciously betrayed his own puzzlement. He pointed out that Roosevelt was "neither a Communist nor a Socialist," any more than he himself was. But "something has taken place in this country — there is some certain kind of foreign 'ism' crawling over this country. What it is I don't know. What its first name will be when it is christened I haven't the slightest idea. But I know that it is here."

Back in January, too, he had referred to the United States as if it were "a foreign land"; in a manner of speaking it had indeed become so — to him.

The election revealed the extent of his alienation. Even the Northeastern cities that had once looked to him for leadership had decisively shifted their allegiance to Roosevelt. Smith could find no explanation for the change but, "You can't lick Santa Claus." So far had he lost the understanding of actuality.

He had always been for the Happy Warrior, remarked an old New York politician; but Smith had "left him out on a limb." Al had taken his walk unaware that no one was following. When he had begun to move apart, the bishops of the National Catholic Welfare Conference were calling for support of the President. Increasingly out of touch with his audience, he had wandered into the isolation of the actor with no stage.

Thereafter, he tended to withdraw from active involvement in public affairs. As a member of the State Constitutional Convention of 1938 he spoke sharply of the need for limiting the taxes on real estate, and maintained a consistent alliance with a handful of anti-New Deal Democrats against Bob Wagner and the party delegation. He was silent on the issue of water power, but condemned the government for throwing money around "the way we used to throw sawdust on the old barroom floor." Perhaps the contrast never struck him between his role then and the part he had played at another convention a quarter-century earlier when he had taken the first steps toward political leadership. Now it no longer seemed to matter.

It was pleasant to get honorary degrees from Columbia, Harvard, N.Y.U. and Catholic University; and to receive Notre Dame's Laetare Medal. He became a trustee of the State College of Forestry, a commissioner of the Palisades Interstate Park and an honorary curator of the Bronx Zoo Every day he walked over to Central Park to watch Joey, his favorite monkey; and at home a hurdy-gurdy ground out "Annie Rooney" and "The Sidewalks of New York."

Housing still seemed important. In 1942, he tried to persuade the New York Life Insurance Company, of which he was a trustee, to rebuild the Oliver Street neighborhood. When that failed, he helped start the state project, later to be named for him.

Mostly, however, other thoughts occupied his mind. The character of his involvement in the Church changed. Never, of course, had his faith wavered. But until the 1930's there had been nothing speculative or introspective about it. He was not interested in the theology of encyclicals. It was simply a natural part of his being and of his situation to perform certain rituals and to accede to certain beliefs. This was no more curious or worthy of explanation than that other men in other situations held other beliefs and acted differently. Religion he had defined essentially as brotherly love, justice and kindness.

In 1928, he had been forced to think about the meaning of his Catholicism — but unwillingly, as if importunate fools were asking questions that needed no answers. The tenor of his response then was that religion was a matter of the private domain of a man's conscience, that it need have no effect at all upon his public role. From that position, on which he had staked his whole career, he could never afford to deviate.

Nevertheless he could not conceal from himself the fact that millions of his countrymen in 1928 and 1932 had thought that Catholicism had disqualified him from the Presidency. And in the shock of that rejection, he was inclined to withdraw to the security of an intimate group, in which he was valued as a Catholic, valued for that which had been the cause of his rejection in the outer, now foreign, world. Then, too, he was aging, and the death of friends turned his thoughts to the eternity that approached. Cut off from politics, he gave his time increasingly to Catholic charities and other lay activities.

In 1937, he visited Europe for the first time and was received by the Pope. "I was never prouder," he said, "than I was today, when I could call him 'Father,' and he called me 'Son.'" In his portrait with the Holy Father, he looks out, with a small boy's wonder, at the mystery of it — not now, as many years ago, at the wide world, but at the wideness beyond the world. A year later he was invested with the dignity and uniform of privy chamberlain in the papal household; he was by then active in the Legion of Decency. Meanwhile, the Fascist revolution in Spain, which aligned the Church against liberalism, futher made Al a stranger in the world of New Deal America. It surprised no one and influenced few when he took another walk in 1940 and supported the Republican candidate for the Presidency.

The crisis of impending war brought him for a time

back on Roosevelt's side. During his European trip he had been distressed by the "tendency among nations to discard democracy and turn to dictatorship for security." Re-affirming his faith in American institutions he had warned: "Too many people today seem to have the idea that the government is the master rather than the servant of the people. They give up liberty in the hope of gaining se-curity, but I am afraid that someday they are going to wake up and find they have lost both." That concern led him, in January 1939, to speak out in favor of the Presi-dent's request for amendment of the neutrality act and thereafter to support Roosevelt's foreign policies. Un-doubtedly Smith helped to counteract isolationist influ-ences among Catholics.

Roosevelt sometimes inquired of their common friends, "How is the old boy?" Al's respect for his rival had not grown; yet with the passage of years, the old bitterness subsided. One day during the war, the President asked Smith to visit the White House and the two men spent an hour laughing at faded memories together. Later, Roose-velt tried to get the RFC to rescue the Empire State Building.

These were gestures without significance. There was not much left to Smith's life. His seventieth birthday passed, marked almost entirely as a family and a Catholic occasion. Soon thereafter, on May 4, 1944, Katie died, and Al lost the constant helpmate whose cheerful solicitude had aided him through all the joys and sorrows of his career.

His own time came before very much longer. Almost at once he began to fail. During the summer he com-plained of intestinal and liver disorders; and early in September he entered St. Vincent's Hospital. On September 25 he was moved to the Rockefeller Institute Hospital. A week later, it became known that he was seriously ill. An Apostolic Benediction came directly from Rome and special prayers were said before Mass in every church of the archdiocese, while the hospital was inundated with telephone calls and visitors. In the early morning of October 4 he died, the immediate cause being "lung congestion and an acute heart condition."

When the news reached Washington, Roosevelt was with his secretary, Grace Tully. The President was saddened as he remembered his relationships with the man who had once been a friend and then an enemy, as he recalled what had been and allowed himself to wonder what might have been. Then, as Miss Tully listened, he reminisced at some length about the "saga of success and service which made the story of Al's life."

For the two hundred thousand Americans who came to St. Patrick's, the somber sheen of thousands of umbrellas held against the October drizzle was symbolic of their own doleful mood. The funeral summoned back memories of a figure out of a past hardly remembered. A decade had changed America almost beyond recognition. But Al Smith after all those years still evoked, for the men and women who waited, themes the significance of which they could only vaguely recapture.

As they thought back beyond the war, beyond the New Deal, there was poignancy in the reminder of what this man had once meant, of what this country had once meant. For it was necessary in 1944 to set in the balance, as against what he had actually achieved, the unfulfillment that had been the tragedy of his life. It was sad and sobering to recall that his failure, after 1928, had in large measure also been a national failure.

Smith's achievements lived long after his death. In New York State his enlightened pioneering in administration had supplied his successors with a firm foundation on which to build and had made the most difficult state the best-governed one in the Union. Page after page in the statute book, as well as magnificent housing projects, a great green park system, and modern hospitals were evidence of his share in awakening the conscience of the nation to the needs of the urban working people. And then, there was a contribution less readily measured — the model of a life of service begun on the East Side, a demonstration that the urban, the immigrant society that had nurtured him was not alien, but a precious part of American life.

Yet a final reckoning had to take account of the failure, also, of the waste of the last fifteen years of his life when his superb abilities had been dissipated in meager criticism. In the larger sense, the failure had been not his alone, but that of his country, for its origins lay in the unwillingness of Americans to meet the challenge he had posed in 1928 and 1932. The effects of failure upon Smith the man were already apparent. But the consequences for the nation were concealed by the depression and the war and would not emerge until after the peace.

Franklin Delano Roosevelt had found it necessary to appeal in the first instance to the agrarians of the West and the South. He had summoned them to battle for social justice and they had responded out of self-interest. But by 1945 it was becoming clear that the farmer's allegiance to the Democratic Party and to the ideals of the New Deal fluctuated with the price of corn and cotton. By then, too, the entrenched power of the Southerners' veto had become a permanent drag on national development.

The weakness of the New Deal, which became apparent only in retrospect, had been to enshrine security as the preeminent social value; liberty was a term all but abandoned to the reactionaries. If the needs of the decade dictated that emphasis, it nevertheless left the masses of people uneducated to the importance of issues wider than their own material safety and well-being. Given the actual conditions of the depression and the intellectual heritage of populism, they were ready to believe, with their political leaders, that all other problems were subsidiary to the economic one, that once the productive system was put in order, every social difficulty would be resolved.

Al Smith had a vague understanding of the deficiencies of that assumption, even in 1934. By the end of the decade he was ready to deny that "security was the essence of freedom." According to that logic, he pointed out, there was no "difference between the president of a large milk company and one of his cows," between "a tom-cat that had eaten twelve canaries and a Russian leader that had stuffed himself with caviar." But his own exile in the Liberty League had immobilized him. Lack of contact with practical problems prevented him either from exploring the implications of his insight or from communicating its importance to a substantial following. Americans would begin to pay the price of that failure in the lush years after 1945, when prosperity once more suffused the economy, but grave social problems remained.

Long after Smith had died, the country would still have to deal with the question raised in the campaigns of 1928 and 1932. Was a Catholic a first-class citizen equal in rights with every other American? The significance of the evasion of that question had been submerged in the 1930's by economic issues. The common misery of the depression had overshadowed the differences between farmers and laborers, between Yankees and Irishmen. But the annoyance never died. There remained a sense of irritating inferiority, sometimes finding an outlet in the reassurance of super-patriotism, sometimes finding expression in resentment of the "conspirators" in Washington who had seized control of the nation, only to betray it. These emotions cropped up in 1936 in the fragmentary vote for Lemke's Union Party, then in the Christian Front and in some aspects of isolationism. The irritation fed off real grievances, such as the archaic systems of representation in many states that discriminated against the cities. It fed also off fancied slights and the fear of persecution. Thus James A. Farley, whose presidential aspirations were frustrated in 1940 and 1944, could find no other explanation for Roosevelt's evasiveness but prejudice. The feeling of irritation influenced most of all the Irish-Americans, but to some extent all the ethnic groups that counted themselves minorities out of a sense of underprivilege.

No national leader of stature offered these people guidance. Their inchoate discontent bubbled dangerously beneath the surface.

Later, with the return of unprecedented prosperity, the economic questions would not seem as important as they had been in the 1930's; and the grievance against inferiority of status would take a more open form. Some of the aggrieved would enlist in the effort through legislation and education to level the barriers of discrimination against all minorities. Others would take a less constructive path, swayed by a hidden animus against the New Deal which, whatever it had done for them, had also killed their leader and extinguished their dreams. They would then stray into the ranks of the McCarthyite rebellion; explain the deficiencies of the New Deal as a Communist conspiracy; and, by their votes in 1952 and 1956, pay back at the expense of Adlai Stevenson debts they felt had been incurred in 1928 and 1932. This would be lingering evidence of an inglorious interlude in American history.

It was the tragedy of Al Smith to have been one of its first victims. A lifetime of effort had brought him, in 1928, to a height from which he glimpsed the promised land of equal opportunity about which generations of Americans had dreamed. From his downfall, millions of his countrymen concluded that it had been only a dream. By 1944, the year of his death, no Catholic or Jew could aspire to be President, whatever other avenues of advance might be open. And, more than a decade after Al Smith's death, it is still a question whether they had truly read or erroneously misread the lesson of his tragedy.

A Note on the Sources

THE WRITTEN WORD did not come as easily to Al Smith as the spoken word. Never a great reader of books, he was always more at ease before an audience than before blank paper. His important communications were face to face. His surviving letters, therefore, are not very communicative and even his speeches suffered through transcription and revision. On the other hand, his state papers as governor are clear, thoughtful and vigorous, reflecting the actual character of his work.

No significant body of Smith's correspondence or collection of his private papers seems to have survived. Fortunately, an abundance of information on the man and his times is available in published sources.

After the defeat in 1928, Smith composed an autobiography, *Up to Now* (New York, 1929), a straightforward narrative of reminiscences, generally reliable in its factual data and revealing the author's attitudes as of the date of publication. Many of his published messages as governor are useful. The more important are collected in his *Public Papers* (2 volumes, Albany, 1920). Others are included in *Progressive Democracy* (New York, 1928). His ideas are also expressed in *Campaign Addresses* (Washington, 1929) and *The Citizen and His Government* (New York, 1935). The talks collected in *Addresses*

. . . *Delivered at the Meetings of the Society of the Friendly Sons of St. Patrick — 1922-1944* (New York, 1945) are particularly important for their intimacy of expression. Addresses and essays on special subjects include *The County Health Unit* (New York, 1927); an introduction to L. H. Pink's *New Day in Housing* (New York, 1928); and a paper on the railroad problem in the National Transportation Committee's *American Transportation Problem* (Washington, 1933).

In the 1920's, Smith set forth many of his ideas in magazine articles. Representative are: "Goals of Government," *Survey,* XLIX (1923), 419; "Housing Policy," *ibid.* XLV (1920), 3. Also worth consulting are: "Spellbinding," *Saturday Evening Post,* CCII (May 24, 1930), 3; "Recollections of My Boyhood Days," *Recreation,* XXXIII (December, 1939), 512. In addition, his contributions to the *New Outlook* (1932-34) were enlightening.

Other works of a governmental nature are of some importance. *The Record of the Constitutional Convention of the State of New York* (4 volumes and appended documents, Albany, 1915) gives the most extensive exposition of Smith's views on government. The *Report of Reconstruction Commission* (Albany, 1919) foreshadows many issues of the next decade. The *Records of the New York State Constitutional Convention* (Albany, 1938) contain information on Smith's later views.

The earlier studies of the man are significant primarily to the extent that their authors had some direct connection with Smith. Emily Warner's *Happy Warrior* (New York, 1956) is thus the account of a devoted daughter often in her father's confidence. Other helpful works include: W. C. Bagley, "Alfred E. Smith's Record in the Promotion of Public Education," *School and Society,* LX (1944), 243; T. H. Dickinson, *The Portrait of a Man as Governor* (New York, 1928); R. L. Duffus, "Al Smith," *Harper's,* CLII (1926), 320; Christian Gauss, "How Governor Smith Educated Himself," *Saturday Evening Post,* CCIV (February 27, 1932), 22; James Kerney, "Personal Portrait of Governor Al Smith," *Scribner's,* LXXX (1926), 242; Robert Moses, "Al Smith," *New York Times*

Magazine, January 21, 1945, 18; Norman Hapgood and Henry Moskowitz, *Up from the City Streets* (New York, 1927) ; Henry Moskowitz, *Alfred E. Smith* (New York, 1924) ; H. F. Pringle, *Alfred E. Smith* (New York, 1927) .

For the general political background, the contemporary press has been most useful. Down to 1917 the newspapers carried far more extensive and more perceptive accounts of the affairs of the state government than they did afterwards. The files of the *Tribune* and the *Times* have been examined with particular care; those of other papers were sampled. From 1917 onward the space devoted in these journals to foreign affairs increased and that given over to local government diminished accordingly. After 1932, the proportion of space devoted to local politics shrank further with the growing focus of press attention on national events. The clippings of the Theater Collection of the New York Public Library and of the Kilroe Tammany Collection at Columbia University proved helpful on special subjects.

Magazines of news and opinion were valuable supplements, especially after 1917. Among the most useful were: *Atlantic Monthly, Collier's, Commonweal, Current History, Current Opinion, Forum, Independent, Literary Digest, Nation, New Republic, Newsweek, Outlook, Review of Reviews, Survey, Time, Vital Speeches,* and *World's Work.*

In a somewhat special category are contemporary observations of local conditions. Among these may be mentioned: the annual reports of the Citizens' Union's Committee on Legislation from 1906 onward; its campaign handbooks and other publications; K. H. Claghorn, "Foreign Immigrant in New York City," *Report of the Industrial Commission,* XV (1901), 149; T. W. Knox, *Darkness and Daylight; or Lights and Shadows of New York Life* (Hartford, 1892) ; C. W. Gardner, *The Doctor and the Devil* (New York, 1894) ; and C. H. Parkhurst, *Our Fight With Tammany* (New York, 1895) on the Parkhurst investigation.

While Smith himself wrote relatively little, he had frequent contacts with men whose records survive in print. The following is a list of those in whose papers or reminiscences he figured or whose writings threw light on his times: James Cannon, Jr., *Bishop Cannon's Own Story* (Durham, 1955) ; Tom Connally, *My Name is Tom Connally* (New York, 1954) ; J. M. Cox, *Journey Through My Years* (New York, 1946) ; J. A. Farley, *Behind the Ballots* (New York, 1938) and *Jim Farley's Story* (New York, 1948) ; E. J. Flynn, *You're the Boss* (New York, 1947) ; Cordell Hull, *Memoirs* (2 volumes, New York, 1948) ; H. L. Ickes, *Secret Diary* (3 volumes, New York, 1953-54) ; J. H. Jones, *Fifty Billion Dollars* (New York, 1951) ; Carroll Kilpatrick, ed., *Roosevelt and Daniels* (Chapel Hill, 1952) ; Louis Marshall, *Selected Papers* (2 volumes, Philadelphia, 1957) ; Charles Michelson, *The Ghost Talks* (New York, 1944) ; Raymond Moley, *After Seven Years* (New York, 1939) ; Robert Moses, *Working for the People* (New York, 1956) ; A. F. Mullen, *Western Democrat* (New York, 1940) ; Frances Perkins, *The Roosevelt I Knew* (New York, 1946) ; W. L. Riordon, *Plunkitt of Tammany Hall* (New York, 1905) : Eleanor Roosevelt, *This I Remember* (New York, 1949) ; F. D. Roosevelt, *Personal Letters, 1928-1945* (2 volumes, New York, 1947-50) and *Public Papers* (13 volumes, New York, 1938-1950) ; D. C. Roper, *Fifty Years of Public Life* (Durham, 1941) ; S. I. Rosenman, *Working with Roosevelt* (New York, 1952) ; Grace Tully, *F.D.R. My Boss* (New York, 1949) . Some of the accounts preserved in the Columbia University Oral History Project also proved valuable.

The period covered by this book has been extensively treated in secondary works, many of which have proved helpful. It has been particularly important as an area of political biography. The following is a list of the more important studies, arranged alphabetically by subject: D. T. Lynch, "Friends of the Governor," *North American Review*, CCXXVI (1928) , p. 420; B. N. Timmons, *Garner of Texas* (New York, 1948) ; R. E. Sherwood, *Roosevelt and Hopkins* (New York, 1948) ; Cleveland Rodgers, *Robert Moses* (New York, 1952) ; Frank Freidel, *Franklin D. Roosevelt* (3 volumes, Boston, 1952-56) ; E. K. Lindley, *Franklin D. Roosevelt* (New York, 1931) ; J. M. Blum, *Joe Tumulty* (Boston, 1951) .

Other secondary works of value include: A. C. Flick, *History*

of the State of New York (10 volumes, New York, 1933-37);
J. A. Friedman, *Impeachment of Governor William Sulzer*
(New York, 1939); Warren Moscow, *Politics in the Empire
State* (New York, 1948), the observations of a veteran Albany
correspondent; H. H. Rosenthal, "Progressive Movement in
New York State" (Harvard University Thesis, 1955); and Ber-
nard Bellush, *Franklin D. Roosevelt as Governor* (New York,
1955) — all on New York State politics. V. A. O'Rourke and
D. W. Campbell, *Constitution-Making in a Democracy* (Balti-
more, 1943) is an account of the convention of 1938. There is
material on the municipality in Allan Nevins and J. A. Krout,
The Greater City (New York, 1948). J. J. Huthmacher,
"Massachusetts Politics" (Harvard University thesis, 1956);
Samuel Lubell, *Future of American Politics* (New York, 1952);
E. A. Moore, *A Catholic Runs for President* (New York,
1956); and R. V. Peel and T. C. Donnelly, *The 1928 Campaign*
(New York, 1931) were helpful on the election of 1928. Walter
Lippmann, *Men of Destiny* (New York, 1927); Raymond
Moley, *Twenty-seven Masters of Politics* (New York, 1949);
A. M. Schlesinger, Jr., *Crisis of the Old Order* (Boston,
1957); and W. A. White, *Masks in a Pageant* (New York,
1928) treated national events.

In the course of the preparation of this work I have acquired
a number of debts to those who knew Al Smith and were able
to supply me with information about him. I am particularly
grateful to Carlos L. Israels, Senator Herbert H. Lehman,
Robert Moses, and Judge Joseph M. Proskauer for having
taken the time to answer my inquiries. For the interpretations
advanced in this book, I am of course solely responsible.

The staffs of the Harvard College Library, of the New York
Public Library, of the Museum of the City of New York and
of the Columbia University Library were most helpful. I
profited also from the efficient secretarial help of Cecily Tour-
tellot, Harriet Dorman, Patricia Will and Rosemary Knapton.
And Mary Flug Handlin has, as in the past, shared all the
labors of research and writing.

O. H.

Index

AS GOVERNOR OF NEW YORK, summary of achievements, 4-5; *1918* and *1920* gubernatorial elections, 71-72; Tammany and other Democratic organizations, 73-74, 92; efficiency of administration, 74-75, 78, 90-98, 110; position on Prohibition, 78-79, 109; religious issue, 79; and the progressives, 81-83; policy toward immigrants, 83-84; patronage, 92; Republican opposition, 94; reorganization of administrative departments, 96-97; improvement in state finances, 98; interest in municipal home rule, 97; tax control, 97-98; natural resources and recreation, 99-100; agricultural problem, 99; utilities issue, 101-102; water power issue, 102-103; social and industrial legislation, 103-108; defense of socialists, 110

PRESIDENTIAL AMBITIONS AND AFTERMATH, religious question raised (*Atlantic Monthly*), 3-4; confidence, 71; dream of Presidency, 112-114; *1924* convention and election, 116-124, 138; recognizing Catholic taboo, 117; attitude toward K K K, 120; *1928* convention and election, 126-138; efforts of Raskob, 128; religious issue, 131-134; personal relations with Roosevelt, 138, 140-145, 153-155, 160-161, 169, 184; position on Prohibition, 152-156; resentment and bitterness, 154-156, 170, 178-179; *1932* convention and election, 157-159, 161-169; ovation at Victory dinner in New York, 159; political isolation and loneliness after election, 170-172; initial approval of Roosevelt adminis-

tration, 172-174; and the New Deal, 174-182; Liberty League, 179; *1936* election campaign, 180; *1940* election, 183-184

BUSINESS ACTIVITIES, Chairman of Board of U. S. Trucking Co., 87; business friends, 87-88; President of Empire State Building, 146, 184; offices in County Trust Company, 147, 149-150; Riordan Suicide, 148; and stock-market crash, 148; County Trust and Mancuso cases, 157; derogatory rumors, 159; member of National Transportation Commission, 170; personal difficulties, 171-172

FINAL YEARS, involvement in church affairs, 182-183; honors and awards, 182; audience with Pope, 183; seventieth birthday, 184; ill health and death, 184-185; Apostolic Benediction, 185; the unfulfillment of his life, 185-186

PRINCIPLES AND CHARACTERISTICS, attention to his dress, 11, 86; Americanism, 62, 79-80, 117, 135; realization of limitations, 66; wit and acting ability, 70; frankness and honesty on Catholicism and his origins, 79, 130; inability to compromise, 79; belief in obligation of government to individual, 80-81, 104, 106; humanitarianism, 82; speechmaking ability, 84-85, 94; love of pets, 86; love of N.Y.C., 88; faith in basic goodness for all, 126; loyal Catholicism, 128, 130, 131; on the Irish, 136; on "forgotten men," 160

Smith, Alfred, Jr. (Alfred's son), 88, 172
Smith, Arthur (Alfred's son), 88